RELATIONAL CHRISTIANITY

Experiencing Intimacy And Companionship With The Living God!

STEVE MEEKS

Calvary Publications
7550 Cherry Park Drive
Houston, Texas 77095
(713) 550-4323

Printed in the United States of America

Library of Congress Cataloging in Publication Data

Meeks, Steve
Relational Christianity: Experiencing Intimacy and
Companionship With The Living God / by Steve Meeks
International Standard Book Number: 0-9630425-0-5
$7.95 Softcover
Library Of Congress Catalogue Card Number: 91-74027

Calvary Publications
7550 Cherry Park Drive
Houston, Texas 77095
(713) 550-4323

ACKNOWLEDGMENTS

My deepest love and heartfelt thanks go to the people of Calvary Baptist Church who have made the journey with me into Relational Christianity. Your encouragement, patience, and prayers have played a vital role in my personal pilgrimage. Also, I want to thank my wife, Sehoy, for her steadfast love and support.

CONTENTS

INTRODUCTION

"Data-based Christianity" was the phrase that came to me as I sought to put into words what I was feeling about my relationship with God. It was Sunday evening and I was the preacher! As I shared my struggle with my congregation, I had a sincere longing to know the nearness of God, but still he seemed distant and uninvolved. My doctrines told me that God was near, but not my heart. My "faith" was summed up in the storing, sorting, and retrieving of information about God. "Data-based Christianity" was an appropriate description of my Christian experience. I seemed to have the right data about God, but it was clear that something was lacking in my relationship with God. That was in 1985. Since that time I have found many other evangelical Christians with similar thoughts and struggles.

On May 26, 1973, I stood at the altar and said, "I do." That was a touching and tender moment as I committed myself to my wife, Sehoy. While that commitment at the altar laid an essential foundation, it was nothing compared to the honeymoon! Nor does it compare to the ongoing experience of intimacy and companionship we have shared over the years. Marriage is not about the ceremony; it is an ongoing relationship between two people in love. So is Christianity. Many evangelicals have stood at the altar and said, "I do" to the Lord. Following that foundational commitment, our relationship with the Lord was replaced by our pursuit of knowledge about the Lord. Rather than experiencing ongoing intimacy and companionship with God, our focus has been on increasing our knowledge of the Bible. That is like a bride being content to hug love letters and kiss photographs, while her bridegroom stands knocking outside the door. Our Heavenly Bridegroom is also knocking, waiting for his bride to open the door. He wants to come in. He longs to fellowship with us.

When Jesus was asked what is the greatest commandment which God has given to man, he answered, in Matthew 22:37-40:

> "'Love the Lord your God with all your heart and with all your soul and with all your mind.' This is the first and greatest commandment. And the second is like it: 'Love your neighbor as yourself.' All the Law and the Prophets hang on these two commandments."

There are many commands, great principles, and spiritual laws contained in the Scripture, but Jesus says they can all be summed up by truly loving God and man. My generation has amassed the information, analyzed, organized, and categorized the truths of God into our doctrines, thinking that is the key to knowing him. We are doing Christianity backwards. It is when one is immersed in a *relationship* with God that the truths of God are unfolded, not just into our doctrines, but into our lives.

It is that relational aspect of Christianity that we have lost. It must be restored. The Father fully intends his children to have intimacy and companionship with himself. He has not left us as orphans. Our minds have been filled with information about God, but our lives have not been filled with the presence of God.

This book is written for those who, like myself, have found their Christian experience somewhat lacking. It has not measured up to what was expected, nor has it matched up with what God has promised. There are many evangelicals who are committed, but disillusioned; searching, but unsatisfied.

It is written for those who are faithful, but weary. Why is it that we are serving Jesus as faithfully as we know how, but we have not found "rest for our souls?" How can we be so committed and yet feel so alone when he promised, "I will be with you always?" We give ourselves to God, to others, and to his church, and yet we feel so empty and drained and dry. Didn't he say something about "rivers of living water" and being "filled to the measure of all the fullness of God?"

We have doctrines for these promises, but we have so very little experience. What good are all our doctrines if they do not work in our lives? What is the point of doctrine if it carries with it no life? Did God really mean those things? Are they meant to be only doctrinal concepts, or are they meant to be a living reality? The Author of Life never intended that our spirituality be reduced to mere mentality. These promises are meant to be more than doctrines, they are meant to be a living experience. They are more than just words, they are our birthright!

We have settled for too little of God's kingdom in our lives. We have come to accept as normal, or at least inescapable, impurity, pressure, and passionless faith. Yet God has declared that his kingdom is "righteousness, peace, and joy in the Holy Spirit" (Romans 14:17).

This book is also written for those who love the church but are somewhat disillusioned with her current expression in our culture. Through all of the talk of renewal over the past two decades, we are still where we were. We seem to be going in circles, functioning as maintenance crews who live out the annual rituals with little or no advancement in maturity and ministry effectiveness. For all our knowledge, *we* are yet unchanged. There is a reason for that: knowledge cannot change us. Only God can change us. In the fall of 1981, I wrote in my doctoral project that "there is a crucial need for a strong *doctrinal* foundation upon which God's people can build their lives and grow their church to the glory of God." Since that time God has slowly, and at times painfully, taught me that there is but one foundation for my life and for the church, and that is the man, Christ Jesus. He is a person. He is a living being. He is not the sum of my doctrines; he is the *author* of my doctrines.

The renewal of the church will not come through mere structural, doctrinal, or methodological changes. The renewal of the church will come through the presence of Jesus being manifested in our midst. When he comes, he makes all things new. He makes old creatures into new creatures; he makes old covenants into new covenants; he makes old wineskins into new wineskins. The person of Jesus is the source of renewal.

There must be a refocusing of our Christian faith.

We must come to experience Christianity as an ongoing, intimate relationship with God. Our informational approach through formulas, self-help principles, and doctrinal instruction has informed us about the Word of God, but it has not infused us with the God of the Word.

The "data-based Christianity" of our western culture has led us into busyness, barrenness, and burnout. There is a vast longing for spiritual reality. There is an increasing thirst for living water. Our longings will not be satisfied and our thirst will not be quenched by seeking answers, but by seeking him. Jesus said, "If any man is thirsty, let him come unto *me* and drink" (John 7:37).

There are many books, old and new, written around the theme of knowing God. After reading many of them, I have found that most deal with knowing God only on the cognitive level. They appear to be "informational" as opposed to "relational." They explain God's attributes, exalt his character, and teach true and wondrous things about God. But there is little about how a person can find intimacy and communion with God other than on the level of rational observation and appreciation. While that is good and helpful, it is also incomplete.

God dwells beyond our concepts, behind our analogies, deeper than our explanations. They all may point to God, but they are not God. He dwells mysteriously, miraculously, and majestically at another level of reality. Has not God himself declared that he is looking for those who will worship him in "*spirit* and

in truth?" Are we not invited to "*taste* the Lord and see
that he is good?" Beneath our rationalizing, God is
there. He is a Living Being. He can be known and
experienced in intimate, personal fellowship. The
concepts, analogies, and teachings of the Scripture have
pointed the way. They provide guideposts and signs
which declare the right road from the wrong ones, but
God is not the signposts. He is the *destination*. He is
the termination, the fulfillment.

   This book is about the One who promised us "life
abundantly." It is about companionship and intimacy
with God. If you are one who longs to be near to him,
then read on prayerfully. I mean that. Pray. Ask God
to speak to you as you read. You will find that he is still
Immanuel, God with us.

RELATIONSHIP
VS
INFORMATION

In December of 1986, I was diagnosed as having a very serious disease. It was a bad news, very bad news situation. The bad news was that I had this disease. The very bad news was that it was communicable and I had given it to others. In fact, I had been giving it to others for years without knowing it. During a week set apart to seek God, the Great Physician came and diagnosed me as having a disease I now call orthodoxitis.

At that time, I was in the middle of a sermon series on how the church was to be a healthy body and a beautiful bride. The people were so receptive and were telling me every week just how much they were learning. But in the quietness of those days alone, the Father impressed upon my heart that the people were learning the truth, but it was not transforming their lives. The messages were filling their minds, but not stirring their souls.

John Wesley said, "Orthodoxy, or right opinion, is

at best, a very slender part of religion. Though right relationships cannot subsist without right opinions, yet right opinions may subsist without right relationship. There may be right opinion of God without either love or a right relationship with Him. Satan is proof of this." It is not that an intellectual understanding of God is unnecessary, it is just inadequate. We have confined our spirituality to the reasoning mind. We have reduced our faith to a matter of thinking, verbalizing, and rationalizing.

The church in America is infected with western rationalism and materialism. We have placed so much faith in our reason that the Living God has been lost. But human reason alone cannot conquer sin and Satan. We must have our eyes opened to the fact that the human mind is also fallen, crippled by sin. When Adam sinned in the garden, we lost not only our *moral* likeness to God, we also lost God's *wisdom*.

The result is that education cannot save us. Only Jesus can save us. All evangelicals acknowledge that only a personal relationship with Jesus will save us. Yet, we turn right around after we are saved and assume that the way to live the Christian life is by acquiring biblical truth and applying it to our lives. We realize the relational aspect of entering our salvation, but we have missed the relational aspect of living out our salvation.

CHRISTIANITY IS RELATIONAL BY NATURE

The New Testament constantly describes our Christian faith in relational terms. There we find that

God is our Father (Matthew 6:9); Jesus is our Elder Brother (Romans 8:29); we are God's children (1 John 3:1); we are a part of God's family (Ephesians 2:19); we are brothers and sisters (James 2:15). The very essence of salvation itself is relationship. John 1:12 says, "Yet to all who received him, to those who believed in his name, he gave the right to become children of God--" The right to become God's kids! What a tender and intimate thing salvation is, not only to us, but to our Father.

Salvation is relational in nature, not informational. When we were born again we did not merely come to a new understanding of God, we entered a new relationship with God. Information was involved, but it is not the Source, nor the Agent, nor the Goal of salvation. Salvation is not understanding and agreeing with four spiritual laws. Salvation is entering into a relationship with the One who decreed the four spiritual laws! It is not the truths that save us, it is submitting to *the Truth*, even Jesus. *He* is the "Author and Finisher of our faith" (Hebrews 12:2).

If we assume any focus for our salvation other than a relationship with God, then we have missed the point. Our relationship with God must also be the focus for *living* the Christian life. The Christian life is not meant to be a pursuit of the information and application of the biblical data. Christian living is supposed to be the pursuit of God. Jesus said in John 17:3, "Now this is eternal life: that they may *know you*, the only true God, and Jesus Christ, whom you have sent."

THE LOSS OF RELATIONSHIP

Our salvation, which began by entering a relationship with God, grows and deepens by cultivating that relationship. When you became a Christian, you didn't do it because you wanted to become a student of the Christian religion, you did it because you wanted and needed to know God. But our western, rational approach to life has subtly deceived us. We have substituted thinking for living. They are not the same thing.

In western culture, we are trained from our earliest days that the ability to store, sort, and retrieve information is the key to success. Every elementary child in America knows it all comes down to regurgitating the information on test day. That same mind set blankets the thinking of the evangelical church in America. Thus, "seekers of God" are those who sit in church week by week to hear lectures on God. We assume that because we are storing more information about God in our minds, we are possessing more of God in our hearts. That assumption is false. Thinking about God is not the same thing as relating to God, which is the purpose of salvation and Christian living. God's desire is to raise a family, not to enroll students. What began as a relationship with God has been lost in our pursuit of information about God. It is this basic flaw in our approach to Christianity that short-circuits many believers from experiencing an intimate relationship with their heavenly Father.

We are continuing to feed from the Tree of

Knowledge of Good and Evil. We have forsaken the Tree of Life. The information we receive from the Tree of Knowledge may all be true, but it does not produce life. Information produces education. Jesus produces life. He is the Tree of Life. It is to him, as a person, we must come, not merely to information about him.

DECEPTIVE SUBSTITUTES

With the loss of relationship, we have settled for some costly and deceptive substitutes in our expression of Christianity. We have substituted *success* for *servanthood.* In trying to be a success by growing a church, engaging in some ministry endeavor, or living for God, we live under the pressure to perform. Not only must we perform, we must achieve certain results. After all, that is the measurement of success. Our Christianity takes on an atmosphere of drivenness, leading only to disappointment, frustration, and a loss of self-worth if we fail to "succeed." Those who "succeed" face a worse fate: they substitute the feelings of success for the peace and joy of knowing the living God.

For many years the focus of my ministry was to be a success for God. Of course, success was measured by the number of people who came to church. When things were going well I felt good about my relationship with God. When things weren't going well my relationship with God was also on the rocks. God has since taught me that my relationship with him is dependent upon my love and obedience to him, not the number of people I can attract. Jesus said,

Whoever has my commands and obeys them, he is the one who loves me. He who loves me will be loved by my Father, and I too will love him and show myself to him (John 14:21).

I have learned that my relationship with God is based upon my love for him, which results in obedience to his commands. In the security of that relationship I can serve God in any situation which he places me. No matter the outward success, big or little, great or small, when I am loving and obeying God, I can be secure, confident, and at peace.

Servanthood brings simplicity. Servanthood is not measured by results; it is measured by obedience. It is lived not in the atmosphere of drivenness and pressure to perform, but in simply being attentive to the Master's voice, available to his call, and obedient to his word. Servanthood is lived in the atmosphere of a relationship with the Master. The person who seeks to be a success is offering to God his work. The one who seeks to be a servant is offering to God himself.

Another deceptive substitute we have made is *construction* for *transformation.* American evangelicals are constantly pushing to *do* something. We are very much like Peter on the Mount of Transfiguration when he wanted to build three tabernacles. It may have been a great project, but it was not the will of God. Peter had good intentions; but good intentions do not guarantee that we are doing the will of God. We are project oriented. We have developed thousands of programs and methods by which we can build the church. We enlist people, get them busy in our projects and programs, and we are convinced that this is Christianity. Much of our activity, however, actually hinders God's true plan. We may end up building our church, but not *his*.

Our goal is not construction, it is transformation. In Matthew 16 Jesus said, "I will build my church." Our part is not building the church, it is *becoming* the church. The Lord is building his church and he is doing it by transforming us! Ephesians 2:21-22 says,

> In him the whole building is joined together and rises to become a holy temple in the Lord. And in him you too are being built together to become a dwelling in which God lives by his Spirit.

We are to become his "dwelling." We are to become "conformed to the image of Christ." We are to become "members of one another." We are to become his bride "without stain or wrinkle or any other blemish." We are to become "a kingdom of priests." There is much we are to become; there is little we are to build. We have substituted busyness for beauty and hurry for holiness. Many of our efforts at building are hampering our progress at becoming. It is in our becoming that God will build his church.

I have pushed and prodded people in almost every way imaginable in order to build the church. I have tried to motivate them with goals, fascinate them with gimmicks, and stimulate them with slogans. I have tried to move people with guilt. I have chastised them for failure and tempted them with rewards, all for the purpose of building the church. Somehow, I believed that the end justified the means. I now realize that the end must determine the means. The end is not production, it is reproduction. My methods have often been attempts at "force-feeding" the sheep and driving them like work animals to perform their duty. I have since learned that healthy sheep will reproduce naturally. As I have learned to lead people to the Chief Shepherd, to his "green pastures" and "still waters," I have watched their love for him reproduce itself in others.

We have also substituted *busyness* for *nearness.* Our society lives in a galvanized hurry. Christians are no different. The busyness of life, even the Christian life, is robbing us of the precious gift of knowing the nearness of God. For many, busyness becomes a fortress from which we defend ourselves from fear and self-examination. There were many times in my life when I spent sleepless nights, worrying over issues and unsolved problems. The busyness of my days were like the walls of a fort under siege, holding back the invading army of fear. At night, when the busyness would cease, the walls would collapse and the invading army would capture its prey.

Busyness is a weak fortress. It provides crumbling walls and an illusion of protection. Some people spend a lifetime fleeing to the false security found in the illusion of busyness. But deep down within they are empty, afraid to take an honest look, fearing it will all turn to ashes in their hands. And it will turn to ashes, if their lives are built upon busyness rather than upon God.

Busyness, ceaseless activity, and constant motion are the narcotics of many lives. Taken in daily doses it is used to anesthetize the fears, the pain, and the loneliness of an empty life. We are addicted to do, rather than to trust. It is simply an attempt to be our own solution, to be our own deliverer, our own god.

Striving, struggling, and straining must cease. We must learn to "be still," to "cease striving" and know that he alone is God. He is our only solution, our only salvation, our only deliverer. He is our fortress, not busyness. It is the idol of self which daily demands the sacrifice of busyness. God calls us to quietness and trust.

> The fruit of righteousness will be peace; the effect of righteousness will be quietness and confidence forever (Isaiah 32:17).

> This is what the Sovereign LORD, the Holy One of Israel, says: "In repentance and rest is your salvation, in quietness and trust is your strength..." (Isaiah 30:15).

We have settled for busyness instead of nearness. God longs for us to live in the awareness that he is near and that we can trust him. Living in the reality of his nearness brings a humble acceptance, a patient working, a submissive spirit, a trusting heart, and a reliant approach. It does not shirk responsibility; it embraces it with a quiet, unharried approach. The worries, anxieties, and pressures which attach themselves to our responsibilities are not really a part of that responsibility. They are the agitations that arise from a soul that does not yet know how to trust. They are symptoms of a lack of dependence upon God. They reveal a heart that still has "self" at the center. Thus, responsibilities disturb the "self" and bubbles of anxiousness rise to the surface of our lives.

The heart which is abiding in God's nearness, and has God at the center, is quiet and trusting. It submerges all its responsibilities into his divine solitude and finds that in him there is peace. "Self" is swallowed up in Christ, and it is "no longer I that lives, but Christ who lives in me...." Christ is not anxious nor harried, fretful nor pressured. But he is responsible and able! That is why "I can do all things through Christ who strengthens me."

We have made many other substitutes. We have substituted rituals for reality, form for substance, enterprise for intimacy, and concepts for life. It is time for the church to rise up, not in revolt to our evangelical heritage, but in love and reality to embrace our God. We should be grateful for the strong foundation our evangelical background has laid. But we must not stop with less than God himself.

LIVING ON A CONCRETE SLAB

Information is not a bad thing. It is one of the necessary ingredients which must be mixed into the concrete of our faith. Many of us poured a proper foundation in our commitment to Jesus. But after our slab hardened and became firm, we have spent the rest of our lives studying the architectural drawings (Scripture), but never putting up a wall. The Bible is the blueprint; it is not the building. *We* are the building! We are the temple of the Holy Spirit. No wonder God doesn't feel at home in many of our lives; who could feel at home living on a concrete slab?

We are to be building an intimate relationship with our heavenly Father. God wants to make his home in your life. That is not a doctrine; it is a living, spiritual reality. We have settled for studying the blueprint, but have failed to become the Lord's living temple. It is not enough to understand the Scriptures; we must cultivate the relationship. We have substituted doctrine for nearness and information for relationship. Thinking we have become wise, we have become fools.

JESUS IS THE ANSWER

It is because of him that you are in Christ Jesus, who has become for us wisdom from God--that is, our righteousness, holiness and redemption (1 Corinthians 1:30).

Jesus is the way into experiencing the living reality of God. In Matthew 28:20, just before his ascension into heaven, Jesus told his disciples, "I am with you always, even to the end of the age." Jesus is a *personal* and *present* God. He is with us right now.

Evangelical Christians believe that Jesus is our way into heaven, but he is more than that, he is our way into *life!* He is the way to experience God and to live out the reality of God's promises.

Second Corinthians 1:20a says, "For no matter how many promises God has made, they are 'yes' in Christ." Our relationship and intimacy with Jesus is the way into actualizing in our *experience* all the promises of God. Let me take one example and let it serve as an illustration of how all God's promises to us can be realized through intimacy with Jesus.

In John 16:33 Jesus says,

> I have told you these things, so that in me you may have peace. In this world you will have trouble. But take heart! I have overcome the world.

In this verse we are promised peace. The question is, even in the face of the trials and tribulations of this world, do you have peace? Would you characterize your heart and mind as peaceful? Philippians 4:7 says, "the peace of God will guard your *hearts* and your *minds*." Is that true of your experience? If not, why not? That is a promise of God to his children.

Many Christians have a doctrine of peace, but they do not experience it. Let me show you why we don't have God's peace and how Jesus is the way to get it. Our approach to having peace in our lives is to work for it by trying to put all our circumstances in proper order. We try to fix everything and everybody to be the way we want them to be, which we think will result in our being at peace. Now none of us have ever accomplished that...but still we try. It leaves us weary, frustrated, and tired, anything but peaceful.

We may "fix" some circumstances. Some of us are better than others at "fixing" circumstances. But the words of Jesus will always remain true, "In this world you will have tribulation." The truth is, we can never fix all our circumstances. We can never put everything in order; therefore, it is fruitless to seek peace by this method. Listen to Jesus again: "In *me* you may have peace." That is the key. Jesus is the way to experiencing the promise of peace.

Peace is just like forgiveness. We do not forgive because we get everything straightened out or "fixed" with someone who has wronged us. We do not forgive because the offender has changed or responded or been "fixed." We live with a *spirit* of forgiveness that is expressed and experienced whether the circumstances change or not. That is the Spirit of Christ in me. It is Jesus in me forgiving those who are unreceptive or unchanged or unrepentant. Thus, I am free to live without bitterness or grudges because I allow Jesus to forgive through me, not because the circumstances get fixed.

On the cross Jesus prayed for those who had wronged him, "Father, forgive them." As I am intimate with Jesus, as my relationship with him is strong, then when I am wronged I turn to him and he prays the same prayer through me. Peace is the same way. We do not experience peace because we get all of our circumstances straightened out, or "fixed." We never will. Yet, we can live in the experience of peace and express peace toward all our circumstances, fixed or not, because we have a spirit of peace. The Spirit of Christ in me is the *source* of peace.

Peace does not come from ordering our circumstances. Thus, I am freed from the tyranny of having to control and manage and fix all my circumstances. There is real liberty in that! Jesus always comes to set us free. "And if the Son sets you free, you are free indeed." I can live in peace, as long as I live "in Christ." As long as my relationship with Jesus is fresh and alive, his Spirit of peace can flow through my life. It is true: "In *me* you may have peace."

Now, let me make a balance statement. That does not mean we lead a laissez-faire lifestyle. We do seek to promote order in our circumstances, just as we would seek proper relationships with those who have offended us. But my forgiveness does not rest on the response of the offender, it rests on *Christ's manifest presence in my life.* Neither does my peace rest on the response of all my circumstances to ordering. My peace rests on my intimacy with Jesus Christ. He is the way to peace. He is the way to experiencing *all* the promises of God in your life.

American Christianity has reduced the gospel to emphasizing doctrine and form, but true Christianity emphasizes Life, Himself. Jesus is the *truth* about that life, not our cultural way of thinking. Jesus is the *way* to that life, not our abilities. In his living presence is peace, for he is the "Prince of Peace." In his living presence is joy, for he is the God of joy. In his presence is love, for "God is love." In him there is hope, for he is the "God of hope." In him there is faith, for he is the "author and finisher of our faith." Jesus is our righteousness, wisdom, and sanctification. Anything and everything we need, he is it. He is the Source of every resource we need. Our responsibility is not to acquire and apply biblical data, it is to abide with him. Many of us have been satisfied with having *information* about Jesus taught to us, but *true Christianity is having the life of Jesus formed in us.*

PASSION FOR GOD

The number one requirement for coming into intimacy and companionship with God is passion for God. That is the solitary key to living in his presence and experiencing his rest. For many years my passion was misplaced. I had a passion for his blessings, for fruitful service, for spiritual knowledge, and for his guidance. I fell into the trap of trying to use my "quiet time" to try and earn "religious brownie points" with which I could purchase God's favors. Or, I attempted to apply spiritual principles by my abilities in order to attain spiritual results. Both of these are attempts to manipulate God, to use him as a power source, a provider, as a means to accomplish my plans. I even made the mistake of calling it "serving God." In reality, I was seeking to have God serve me by blessing my plans, agendas, and desires.

The journey into knowing God intimately must

begin with passion for God himself. David was a man who knew that passion: "As the deer pants for streams of water, so my soul pants for you, O God. My soul thirsts for God, for the living God. When can I go and meet with God" (Psalm 42:1-2)? Moses knew it: "Then Moses said, 'Now show me your glory'" (Exodus 33:18). Paul knew it:

> What is more, I consider everything a loss compared to the surpassing greatness of knowing Christ Jesus my Lord, for whose sake I have lost all things. I consider them rubbish, that I may gain Christ...I want to know Christ and the power of his resurrection and the fellowship of sharing in his sufferings, becoming like him in his death (Philippians 3:8,10).

Passion involves emotion. Our culture has robbed us of our genuine, God-given emotions. If we are to know God fully, we must love him not only with our minds and our wills, but also with our emotions. Emotions are also a part of God's image in us. He created them. They reflect something of himself. Because of our mistrust of emotions and our overreaction to the abuse of emotions, we have come to possess a passionless faith and a dead orthodoxy. Knowing God must involve our head and our hearts, our thoughts and our emotions, our doctrine and our spirits.

I am not advocating empty emotionalism in which our flesh works up or pretends something that isn't real. I am advocating that we ask God to restore our God-given capacities to experience and express the emotional part of our nature which was created in his image.

God cherishes genuine emotions. Psalms 51:17 says, "The sacrifices of God are a broken spirit; a broken and contrite heart, O God, you will not despise." Have you ever had a broken heart without emotion involved? That would be a contradiction in terms. Yet, it is that brokenness which God will not "despise." In other words, he *esteems* it. He cherishes it and draws near to it. Psalm 34:18 says he is "close to the brokenhearted."

True worship is to be expressed by drawing near to God with thanksgiving and entering "his courts with joy" (Psalm 100:4). Joy, if it has meaning at all, must be endued with emotional content. We had a couple who joined our church that said, "For so long, going to church felt like we were just doing our duty. Now it is refreshing and exciting." We are not to draw near to God merely out of duty; we are to *"delight"* ourselves in the Lord (Psalm 37:4).

Paul taught and ministered with great fervency and emotion. "I served the Lord with great humility and with tears, although I was severely tested by the plots of the Jews...So be on your guard! Remember that for three years I never stopped warning each of you night and day with tears" (Acts 20:19,31). Either Paul was a great actor, a hypocrite, or he experienced and expressed godly emotions.

Jesus, the very Son of God, modeled for us godly emotions in his relationship with the Father. In Luke 10:21 we see Jesus full of joy. Luke 19:41 says, "As he approached Jerusalem and saw the city, he *wept* over it."

Hebrews 5:7 teaches us that, "During the days of Jesus' life on earth, he offered up prayers and petitions with *loud cries* and *tears* to the one who could save him from death, and he was heard because of his reverent submission." Not only did Jesus display his God-given emotions, God honored them.

We must go to the Scriptures again and ask God to open our eyes to the emotional content of our natures, and how they endear us to the Father. The deadness of duty must be replaced with the delight of the Lord. The words of our rituals must be replaced with the life of our relationship. For too long, we have accepted as normal hard hearts and empty spirits. It is time to cry out for hearts of flesh and spirits filled with the fullness of God.

Passion for God does not consist of weak, dull, lifeless wishes and notions concerning God which carry no fervency, zeal, and love. We are living in a self-imposed prison of indifference. We need to become men and women of fire and emotion and zeal.

The first step on the pathway to passion is repentance. We must ask God to forgive us for embracing such a passionless faith and lifeless love. In Revelation 3:19 the Lord calls out to his church in Laodecia, "Those whom I love I rebuke and discipline. So be earnest, and repent." That word "earnest" or "zealous" literally means "boiling with heat." His call for repentance includes fervency, heat and emotion. This is in contrast to the *lukewarmness* of their religion. "I know your deeds, that you are neither cold nor hot. I wish you were either one or the other" (Revelation 3:15)!

Are you on fire for God, or are you an ice cube? If we took a survey, I believe the average evangelical Christian would answer, "Well, I'm not exactly on fire for God. But I'm not an ice cube either!" Where does that leave us? About lukewarm? "So, because you are lukewarm--neither hot nor cold--I am about to spit you out of my mouth" (Revelation 3:16). The bondage of lukewarmness must be broken. It is time for the church in America to rekindle her passion for the Living God and return to her first love.

EXPERIENCE VS KNOWLEDGE 2

In the context of our western, rational culture we often equate knowledge with experience. When we have a knowledge of something, we tend to think we possess the reality. We have come to place intellectual understanding in the same category with experience. Knowledge and experience, however, are not the same thing.

A young man may read every book there is to read on marriage, know all the principles of communication, sharing, and intimacy, but until he's married, he doesn't know the half of it! Knowledge and experience are two very different things. All of his learning may be very beneficial, but it must not be equated with the experience of marriage. He may feel like he knows everything there is to know about marriage. But for all of his "knowledge," he still does not know intimacy, tenderness, companionship, or confrontation. These things are the substance of marriage; knowledge is but the shadow.

We must stop being afraid of experience. In fact, we must reach out to embrace the Living God who is the *Author of all experience.* Our intellectualized Christianity is robbing us of God. Let me assure you, I am not against the use of our intellect. That, too, is a part of God's image in us. What I am against is the divorcing of intellect from experience, just as I am opposed to divorcing experience from intellect. The error for some today is to seek experience apart from understanding. That is dangerous and leads to many abuses. The opposite error, and one of the chief errors of evangelicals, is to seek understanding apart from experience. Both are perversions of the truth.

SUBSTITUTING DEFINITIONS FOR REALITY

The confusing of knowledge for experience has robbed us of intimacy and companionship with God. We have settled for definitions, while God is offering us life. Experience contains life; knowledge contains words. Experience contains emotion; knowledge contains concepts. Experience is relational; knowledge is informational. Yes, knowledge must inform our experience; but it must not *replace* it. If all we have are our ideas about God, then we've missed God.

Jesus made many precious promises to those who would follow him. He has promised "rest for your souls" (Matthew 11:28), "peace" (John 16:33), "life abundantly" (John 10:10), "power from on high" (Luke 24:49), along with many other wonderful things. We have doctrines for all these things, but we have little or no experience of them. For most believers, these things remain untasted concepts.

Psalm 34:8 tells us to *"Taste* and see that the LORD is good." 1 Peter 2:3 teaches us to long for more "now that you have *tasted* that the Lord is good." Taste is an experiential word. If a person has never tasted chocolate, I defy you to explain to him what it tastes like. You may be able to tell him the ingredients, but you cannot explain the taste. Yet, by *experience,* we even know what "dark" chocolate tastes like as compared to "milk" chocolate or "white" chocolate. Experience runs deeper than knowledge. Taste is based on experience, not information.

So it is with knowing God. We may know the words of God's promises: "peace that passes understanding," "love that surpasses knowledge," and "joy unspeakable," but words do not contain life. Jesus contains life. We know the doctrine of those things, but often we do not know the experience. We have settled for knowing the recipe instead of eating the cake!

God means for us to have the reality of what he promises, not merely an intellectual understanding. He is the Author of Life, not a textbook. 1 Corinthians 4:20 says, "For the kingdom of God is not a matter of talk but of power." God has power to bring comfort to those who mourn, praise in the place of despair, affirmation instead of condemnation, love in the place of fear, and life in the place of death (Isaiah 63:1-3; Romans 8:1; 1 John 4:16-18; John 11:25-26).

EXPERIENCE IS NOT A DIRTY WORD

One day I was writing in my journal and I was complaining to God about some of my brothers who base their theology on their experience. Like a lightning bolt from heaven, God spoke clearly to my heart and said, "Yes, Steve, and you base your theology on your *lack of experience!"* Seeking knowledge without experience leads to a lot of doctrine but little life, little love, and no power.

One reason many of us are afraid of spiritual experience is because of the abuses and bad models to which we have been exposed. The fakes, frauds, and fanatics will always be with us. Our response has often been to opt for the easy, less risky way which seeks religious knowledge but rejects spiritual experience. But the answer to abuse is correction, not rejection. There are doctors who are "quacks" and lawyers who are charlatans. If we were to reject all doctors and lawyers because of the "bad apples" we would lose something very valuable. The same is true when we reject spiritual experience because of abuses and bad models.

Experience must be restored to our faith or we will continue to produce a cosmetic Christianity. I want to be clear. I am not saying we are to seek experience. I am saying we are to *seek God.* When you find him, it will be an experience. God expresses himself in a multitude of wondrous ways, but all contain experience. When we encounter the reality of God, we may have an experience of conviction and repentance, or joy and praise, or comfort and hope, or love and adoration. He may touch us with peace, or power, or a sense of his awesome presence. But however it comes, the touch of God will be more than information; it will be an experience.

In July of 1989, our church was just settling in to hear the sermon during our early service. As I stood to preach, the presence of God seemed very real in the room; there was a corporate sense of his nearness. I realized it would not be appropriate for me to preach, but I felt as if one of our associate pastors was supposed to say something. I turned to him and asked, "Do you have something you're supposed to say?" He broke down and began to weep. From that moment, the Spirit of God fell on our congregation with the convicting and saving power of God. People everywhere began to weep. Some began to move to the altar under deep conviction of sin. God was calling us to repentance. That experience began about 8:30 am and lasted until 2:30 that afternoon. We never dismissed for Bible study; those arriving for our second service came into the auditorium and immediately fell under that same power of conviction and repentance. No sermon was preached, no testimonies were given, no offerings were received, but the presence and power of God was experienced. Seventeen people gave their hearts to Jesus Christ that day.

We must not settle for less than the experience of God. When a young man is searching for the girl of his dreams, or a young lady for her Prince Charming, he or she does not consider the journey complete because of reading about that person in a book! Any lover knows the difference between knowledge and experience. Let us remember, "God is love." He prefers lovers to students.

THE TRUTH SHALL SET YOU FREE

In John 8:32 Jesus said that, "You will know the truth, and the truth will set you free." The truth of God is not meant to inform us; it is meant to transform us. Any of God's truth that does not transform us is not really known at all. The equating of knowledge with experience in our culture has led us into deception. We think that because we know something, it is true of us.

Many Christians have a knowledge of the doctrine that we are to be witnesses for Christ. But their lives are actually counter-productive for the cause of Christ. Most evangelicals have a knowledge of the doctrine that Jesus promised "rest" for our souls (Matthew 11:29), but they are full of weariness, frustration, and anxiety. Doctrinal knowledge can be possessed without the truth setting us free. A person truly "knows" a doctrine only when it is a part of their experience, and not until then.

It is one thing for me to teach that Christians are the "sweet aroma" of Christ everywhere they go (2 Corinthians 2:14); it is another for them to be it. *It is doctrine when we believe we are the "sweet aroma" of Christ; it is truth when other people believe it.* Just because we possess the doctrine of being the "sweet aroma" of Christ does not mean that we *are* the "sweet aroma" of Christ. In fact, the only doctrines we really possess are those doctrines which *possess us.*

In order to come into the liberating truths of God, we must stop asking how much we know, and start examining how we live. We are raping the truth with our intellects when we rob the truth of its transforming power by confining it to our collection of doctrines. The living faith which God intends is often aborted by the deception of equating knowledge with experience. Doctrines not lived and experienced deceive us. James said it this way, "Do not merely listen to the word, and so deceive yourselves. Do what it says." Again, in James 2:17, "In the same way, faith by itself, if it is not accompanied by action, is dead." Much of our evangelical faith has come forth stillborn.

LOVING THE TRUTH

There is another subtle deception which the Father uncovered in my heart that helped me move into the liberating power of God's truth. There is a part of our western mindset that clings to skepticism. It causes us to withhold ourselves until there is "convincing proof." I used to pray, "Father, I want to believe, but I need more evidence, because I love the truth. I am going to 'examine everything carefully and hold to that which is good.'" That didn't sound too bad; in fact, it sounded biblical. But one day the Father impressed upon me that I had pushed that part of my mind too far. It was out of balance. He showed me that this part of my mind did not "love the truth," it loved *understanding* the truth. The Father went on to remind me that the Truth is a Person, even Jesus. Jesus said, "I am the truth"

(John 14:6).

Since Jesus is the Truth, I can never fully understand the truth because his ways are higher than my ways and his thoughts are higher than my thoughts (Isaiah 55:8-9). Romans 11:33 says, "Oh, the depth of the riches of the wisdom and knowledge of God! How unsearchable his judgments, and his paths beyond tracing out!" Ephesians 3:19 tells us that his love "*surpasses* knowledge." Philippians 4:7 teaches us that his peace "*transcends* all understanding." Every attribute of Jesus, in its fullness, is beyond our comprehension. What does that mean for us? It means that, ultimately, a love for the truth means obedience to Jesus, not understanding.

In the Garden of Eden, man was not created to live by his knowledge of good and evil. That was the very thing he was commanded to avoid. Man and woman were meant to live from the Tree of Life, which meant *trusting and obeying* what God had said, whether they understood or not. As we try to live by seeking proof, examining data, and loving understanding, rather than the Truth himself, we too are cut off from our intimacy with God.

Am I saying that we are to cast our brains to the wind? No. I am saying we are not to exalt our intellect above the voice of God. We are not to sit in judgment over what God says. We are to hear the voice of our Master and then we are to trust and obey whether we understand or not. "My sheep listen to my voice; I know them, and they follow me" (John 10:27).

The purpose of God revealing himself is never to give convincing proof. God could convince the whole world of his reality and the Lordship of Jesus in a split second if he chose to do so. *The purpose of revelation is not convincing a person's mind, but testing a person's heart.* When God comes to sow the seed of his revelation in one's heart, the issue is not whether the seed is good or bad. The issue is the condition of the heart. The hard heart will have the seed snatched away by the enemy. The shallow heart will not allow the seed to take root. The preoccupied heart will choke out the seed with other concerns. But the good heart will receive and experience the life of God. (See Luke 8:4-15.)

We have been so focused on data, information, and proof, that we have forgotten to examine the condition of our own hearts. Our preoccupation with knowledge and evidence has caused us to overlook the real issue. Is my heart receptive to God? I am not asking if it is receptive to *understanding* God. I am asking if it is receptive to trusting, obeying, and loving him.

The heart that trusts and obeys is the one which loves the Truth. "Whoever has my commands and obeys them, he is the one who loves me. He who loves me will be loved by my Father, and I too will love him and show myself to him" (John 14:21). That heart is the one which will be set free. "If the Son sets you free, you will be free indeed" (John 8:36). It is the heart which loves Jesus that will experience the promises and the presence of God.

THE LOSS OF GOD

Real Christianity is more than an intellectual attempt to master certain ideas about God. It is more than thinking about spiritual things. *Christianity is a relational experience.* Having a knowledge about God is totally different from living in fellowship with God. As religious people, we fool ourselves into thinking that because we have a head full of beliefs, we have a heart full of God. This is not so. If we look closely and honestly, our experience tells us it is not so.

In the process of learning to relate to God, I slowly began to realize the lack of experiential reality in my doctrines. At one point in the journey I recorded the following thoughts:

> To know something intellectually, to believe it, is not the same thing as experiencing it. Some things I thought I knew, I did not know at all. I intellectually believed and volitionally embraced the doctrines of Christianity, but I was not experiencing their reality. In the past few weeks I have begun to experience the reality of some of the things I have believed and embraced for many years. For years I have studied, taught, preached, and assumed I was living these truths. All the while, there was a nagging feeling that "if what I have is it, then the Bible states its case a bit strongly." I understood the doctrine of these truths, yet in comparison with the Scriptures, something was lacking in my experience. The

Scriptures promised "rest" (Matthew 11:28), "rivers of living water" (John 7:37), and "the fullness of God" (Ephesians 3:19). When I compared my *beliefs* with these things, that was okay. When I compared my *life* with them, it did not match. Because of what I knew, I assumed I possessed the reality. What I have found is that being content with my knowledge actually prevented me from going on to experience the reality. I was satisfied that my beliefs were right. I was satisfied that I had a reasonable grasp of the scriptural teachings. It was not until God brought me to a point where I was utterly *dissatisfied with my experience,* that I became receptive to seeking the reality behind my knowledge. It was not that what I knew was wrong, it was just inadequate. What I knew was surface, it was external, it was lacking in spiritual depth and transforming power.

Our shallow lives belie the reality of our doctrines. Often, our response is to water down our doctrines to conform with our lack of experience. We take truths like "abiding in Christ," or "being filled with the Spirit," and relegate them to the realm of knowledge. They cease to be a living experience and become an indication of how much we know. This process is robbing us of fellowship with the living God and his presence in our lives.

We have tried to contain God in concepts. But God cannot be grasped with our thoughts. All of our concepts have limits. To define an idea is to give it boundaries. What meaning would there be to the game of basketball if there were no boundaries, no rules, and no baskets? Concepts and boundaries are necessary for meaning. Since God is infinite, he has no boundaries. Therefore, there is no thought, no concept that can contain him. So any ideas, any doctrines we have of God (i.e. God is "just," God is "righteous," God is "love") are only analogies; they are not the person of God. They may be true analogies, but in grasping the analogy we have failed to grasp God, the one whom we seek.

What am I saying? I am saying that there is no thought about God that can contain him. I am saying that you can know *about* God through concepts and doctrines, but you can only *know God* through *experience*. When our faith has degenerated into merely *thinking* about God and *talking* about God, then we have lost God.

You do not have to be a nutritionist to enjoy a good steak. You don't grill a steak for the purpose of analyzing its ingredients. You don't grill a steak in order to have a lesson on proteins. But that is what we're doing with God. We are analyzing, but we are not relating.

Don't misunderstand me. We are not to reject our concepts as lies, but we must not cling to them, as if having *them* is the same thing as having *him*. Our concepts of God are like the runway upon which an airplane travels. They are necessary. But at some point you must lift off from the concepts into fellowship with God. We must move beyond knowledge into experience.

WHAT ABOUT THE BIBLE?

The God of the Bible is a Living Being. He is a Personal Being. He reveals himself to men. In John 1:1 we read, "In the beginning was the Word, and the Word was with God, and the Word was God." What is a word? It is a means of communication. Since the Word is God, that means it is part of God's nature to communicate. God desires to express himself, to reveal himself to men.

One of the ways God expresses himself is through the Bible. It is a form of communication from God. Let me say that I believe the Bible is the infallible, authoritative Word of God. But the Bible is not God. He exists apart from the Bible. If he had never given us the Bible, he would still exist.

God gave us the Bible in order to express or reveal himself to men. *The Bible was never meant merely to inform us about God, it was meant to lead us to God.* When you go to the grocery store and buy a can of green beans, you know what is in the can because of what the label tells you. When you get home, you don't cook the label and serve it to your kids! The label merely describes the contents. That is what the Bible does for us. It tells us what God is like. But, it is not God. The Bible describes for us how God and humans are to relate with each other; but knowing the Bible is not the same thing as knowing God.

We have lost our living relationship with God when our faith consists of merely pursuing biblical information. Even if you are taking that information and trying, to the best of your abilities, to apply it to your life, you can still miss God. The accumulation and application of data, even data from God, can occur entirely as an effort of an individual's intellect, willpower, and flesh.

In John 5:39-40 Jesus says, "You diligently study the Scriptures because you think that by them you possess eternal life. These are the Scriptures that testify about *me*, yet you refuse to come to *me* to have life." We need to pay close attention to what Jesus is trying to teach in these verses. What he is saying is that *knowing the Scriptures does not give life. Jesus* gives life! The Jewish leaders to whom Jesus was speaking in John 5 knew the Scriptures. They studied the Scriptures. But they did not know Jesus.

We may study the Scriptures diligently, but the real issue is this: how well do we know Jesus? Jesus is the source of life, not the Scriptures. Jesus is the *source* of wisdom, not the Bible. Knowing the Scripture does not produce holiness. Jesus produces holiness. Don't misunderstand me. Jesus will use the Bible. The Scripture is one of his tools. But *he* is our "wisdom from God--that is, our righteousness, holiness and redemption" (1 Corinthians 1:30).

When we open the Bible we must do more than interpret doctrine; we must interact with a Person. It is not our doctrines of God that transform us, it is the God of our doctrines. It is focusing on a person, and our relationship with him, that changes our lives. "All authority in heaven and on earth" was not given to a Book; it was given to Jesus. It is our fellowship with him that makes the Bible what God meant it to be. Turn your time in the Bible into dialogue with Jesus. Interact with him. Set your affections on him. He has promised to "be with you always."

We must be careful to remember that we can be "always learning but never able to come to the knowledge of the truth" (2 Timothy 3:7). Jesus is the Truth, and the Way, and the Life. Our informational society needs to be careful to heed the admonition of the apostle Paul when he said, "Knowledge puffs up, but love builds up" (1 Corinthians 8:1).

RELATIONAL CHRISTIANITY VS CULTURAL CHRISTIANITY

3

Our journey into knowing God calls for more than information; it calls for a relationship. Our relationship with God requires more than knowledge; it requires experience. Refocusing our Christian faith can come only through the grace of God. Several vital issues must be addressed before we can enter into "Relational Christianity."

The Spirit of Truth must guide us, speak to us, and touch both our hearts and our minds. Refocusing our Christian faith cannot be done purely by instruction; there must also be illumination. 1 Corinthians 2:9-12 says,

> However, as it is written: "No eye has seen, no ear has heard, no mind has conceived what God has prepared for those who love him" -- but *God has revealed it to us by his Spirit.* The Spirit searches all things, even the deep things of God.

For who among men knows the thoughts of a man except the man's spirit within him? In the same way no one knows the thoughts of God except the Spirit of God. We have not received the spirit of the world but the Spirit who is from God, *that we may understand* what God has freely given us.

Paul knew our need of illumination by God's Spirit. In Ephesians 1:17-19 he prays,

I keep asking that the God of our Lord Jesus Christ, the glorious Father, may give you the *Spirit of wisdom and revelation, so that you may know him better.* I pray also that the *eyes of your heart may be enlightened* in order that you may know the hope to which he has called you, the riches of his glorious inheritance in the saints, and his incomparably great power for us who believe.

We must acknowledge our need and our lack of wisdom. We must ask the Holy Spirit to teach us, quicken us, and stir our hearts with love for God. He delights in doing it. Ask him. Ask him every day.

The intellectual pursuit of God will not cause God to disclose himself to you. God looks on our hearts. Our search for intimacy and companionship with the Living God must issue from our hearts, not our heads. "You will seek me and find me when you seek me with all your heart" (Jeremiah 29:13). God promises that those who hunger and thirst for him will find him.

Passion for God himself is the only motivation that will bring you into the discovery of his nearness. The one who has a heart for God will find the heart of God.

WHAT IS RELATIONAL CHRISTIANITY?

Defining relational Christianity is like trying to nail Jello to a tree. Every time you think you've got it, something slips away. There are many components of relational Christianity that are difficult to define even in human relationships. We may seek to use technical terms and phrases to describe love, intimacy, companionship, and friendship, but no description can capture the life which is involved.

Relational Christianity is about living life in intimate companionship with God. It is being aware of his nearness, sensing his love, and giving him yours. It results in deep trust, abiding peace, and tender fellowship. It brings to us in experience what our traditional faith gave us only in words.

CULTURE'S CARICATURE

Western culture has given us a caricature of true Christianity. Our culture's model of Christianity is based on rationalism and pragmatism. We have even boiled the gospel down to a "do-it-yourself" kit. We give people information about God, information about man's need, and information about Christ's remedy. Our rationalism says, "understand it" and our pragmatism says, "apply it." So they pray the prayer, get baptized, and start going to church. We are not leading them to *him*, we are leading them to *it* (the gospel). But "it" does not transform their lives. We are trying to apply the gospel by our own power, from the outside in. But the gospel is not *our* "power unto salvation," it is "the power of *God* unto salvation" (Romans 1:16). When we come to him, he applies the gospel to us, and he does it from the inside out.

Our cultural solution to non-transformed "converts" is discipleship. Discipleship, in our culture, means education. We seek to indoctrinate them by filling them with biblical information which they can apply to their lives. This approach causes people to rely on their intellect and willpower, but not on the Living God. The result is a data-based religion and a dead orthodoxy. We have come to depend on principles instead of prayer, programs instead of power, formulas instead of faith, and gimmicks instead of God.

In Jeremiah chapter two, the Lord asks why his people had strayed so far from him (v.5). Then in verse six, and again in verse eight, he said that neither the people nor the priests bothered to ask, "Where is the Lord?" Neither is the church today asking, "Where is the Lord?" She is asking, "How can we grow bigger?" A few years ago the pastors of our church were on a calendar planning retreat. We had just finished the calendar for the coming year and I said, "Whew! I'm glad that's over." As we looked over the year's worth of activities and events (which looked almost identical to the prior year), one of the men asked, "Is this what Jesus died for?"

That is a worthy question to ask of our lives and our churches. Where is the Lord in the midst of our busyness, our weariness, and our yearly ritual of activities? The Lord's verdict in Jeremiah 2 was, "My people have committed two sins: They have forsaken me, the spring of living water, and have dug their own cisterns, broken cisterns that cannot hold water" (v.13). We have dug our own broken cisterns. We have taken the shovels of rationalism and pragmatism provided by our culture and we have dug cisterns of information and organization. What we don't have are "rivers of living water" flowing from our innermost being. Yet, that is the promise of the Lord for those who come to him. He is the "spring of living water" that produces the rivers in us. It is time for us to honestly ask, "Where is he?"

THE CHRISTIAN'S REAL IDENTITY

One aspect of refocusing our faith is to turn the lens upon ourselves. One reason we have lost the nearness of God is that we are not living out his plan. We are blazing our own trails, or following the trails of others into the Christian faith. All pathways but his will lead us into a dead end alley. What does it really mean to follow Jesus? What was Jesus' intention when he called me to himself?

When Jesus calls people to himself, he does not call learners, he calls *trainees*. While learning is certainly a part of being trained, it must be viewed as a means and not the end. Matthew 4:19 says it clearly: "Come, follow me," Jesus said, "and I will make you fishers of men." Jesus recruited, trained, and commissioned the twelve. The twelve enlisted the seventy (Luke 10:1-2). The seventy reached the one hundred and twenty (Acts 1:15). The one hundred and twenty reached three thousand (Acts 2:41). The process is one of enlisting trainees to go into the harvest. Do you see yourself as one of the trainees of Jesus? We have been ensnared by our culture into thinking about Christianity rather than doing it. We have become learners instead of disciples, students instead of servants.

Another of Jesus' intentions was to assemble an *army,* not an audience. 2 Timothy 2:3-4 tells us to "Endure hardship with us like a good soldier of Christ Jesus. No one serving as a soldier gets involved in civilian affairs--he wants to please his commanding officer." Jesus calls us to war against the kingdom of darkness. We are to "fight the good fight of faith," overcome the "gates of hell," and stand firm against the "schemes of the devil." He is not interested in a large number of fans; he is seeking a loyal group of followers. Our culture has polluted us with an audience mentality which must be demolished before we will become the army of God.

The Lord even provides armor for us to wear in the battle (see Ephesians 6:10-18). If an individual belongs to Jesus they can't dodge the draft and there are no deferments. Our armor includes no "back-plate of cowardice," "bunk bed of indifference," or "force-field for the uncommitted." The presence of God will only be experienced when a soldier reports for active duty.

Jesus also intended that those who follow him are

to be *ambassadors,* not agreers. "We are therefore Christ's ambassadors..." (2 Corinthians 5:20). An ambassador is one who lives in another country and represents the will of the one who sent him there. He is not there to represent his own will or desires, but the will of the one who has given him his assignment. We have not been called to merely agree with the teachings of Jesus. He is not looking for apologists who will confirm his will, he is looking for ambassadors who will carry out his will. When confronted with the word and will of God, we are not merely to listen to it, we are to do it.

If we are going to come to know the daily presence and companionship of God, then we must "be about our Father's business." Jesus said, "The one who sent me *is with me;* he has not left me alone, *for I always do what pleases him"* (John 8:29). Jesus constantly knew the presence of the Father because he was consistently doing the works of the Father. Jesus promises that what was true for him will also be true for us: "Whoever serves me must follow me; and *where I am, my servant also will be.* My Father will honor the one who serves me" (John 12:26). We have not been called to learn about Christianity. We have not been called to talk about Christianity; we have been called to live it.

AN EMERGING MODEL

What does relational Christianity look like in a church setting? How is it expressed? What I am about to share with you is one example of living out a relational model of Christianity within the local church setting. These are not theoretical conjectures. They have been lived out in the crucible of experience. I am quite certain we do not have the full wisdom of God, but we do have a viable expression of relational Christianity. We are looking for others who will rise up and serve as models to us, drawing us even closer to the One we love.

Please permit me a word of personal testimony. I was raised in a traditional, evangelical church. I pastored two traditional churches for almost ten years. I am thankful for the foundation which the traditional church laid in my life. While I am thankful for its strengths, I must not be blind to its weaknesses. I believe the traditional church has stopped short of God's design. I am not against any church. I am for the church. But I am for the church being the church as God intends for it to be. I am committed to the renewal and revitalization of the church that it might be the healthy body and the beautiful bride of Jesus.

Now I want to draw some contrasts between the traditional church and a church which embraces relational Christianity. There must be a definite shift in philosophy and practice of ministry if a church is to experience relational Christianity. These contrasts do not represent any individual church, but are reflective of the church as a whole. I also recognize that the following contrasts do not represent absolute categories. They represent categories at opposite ends of a sliding scale. It is my observation that the traditional church tends to operate on the informational end of that scale.

THE TRADITIONAL MODEL IS INFORMATIONAL

THIS MODEL IS RELATIONAL

Matthew 22:37-40

Jesus replied: "'Love the Lord your God with all your heart and with all your soul and with all your mind.' This is the first and greatest commandment. And the second is like it: 'Love your neighbor as yourself.' All the Law and the Prophets hang on these two commandments."

Many times the traditional church produces data-based Christians who are good at sorting, retrieving, analyzing, and organizing the biblical information. The result is believers who are pumped full of biblical truth but do not experience that which they believe. Many such believers have made their goal reading the Book, or understanding the Book, or teaching the Book. They think that is Christianity.

The Book is meant to lead you into the *experience* of God who wrote the Book! We are to live in a personal, loving, intimate fellowship with God. That does not mean that doctrine is unimportant; it is just inadequate. It should serve as a sure foundation, but it must not become an end unto itself. The information about God is not our goal. God is our goal. Therefore, this approach seeks not to have a data-based Christianity which merely increases biblical knowledge, but to have a love-based Christianity which develops a personal relationship with the Most High God.

THE TRADITIONAL MODEL IS BASED ON EDUCATING

THE RELATIONAL MODEL IS BASED ON EQUIPPING

Proverbs 27:17

As iron sharpens iron, so one man sharpens another.

The educational approach gives people instructional information about ministry and then expects them to do it. People are told "how to" do it. They are given principles and methods and then told to apply them to their lives.

Jesus' method of equipping disciples was not to say here is "how to" do it, but rather, "Follow me" (Matthew 4:19). He modeled for them the perfect life of a servant of God. Our lives may not be perfect, but modeling is still the best method of equipping disciples. You aren't equipped for ministry just because you've had a class or just because you studied the book. You don't become a football player just by studying the play book. You become a football player by putting on the pads, doing the exercises, taking the field, and running the plays. It's not enough just to attend classes. You are equipped by doing. You learn to minister by ministering. It is not enough to *know* what your teacher knows, you must *do* what your teacher does. In Luke

6:40 Jesus said, "A student is not above his teacher, but everyone who is fully trained will be like his teacher." Again, in John 14:12, he says, "I tell you the truth, *anyone* who has faith in me *will do* what I have been doing...." To be *educated* means you have the *knowledge*. To be *equipped* means you have the *know-how*.

THE TRADITIONAL MODEL IS PROGRAM-ORIENTED

THE RELATIONAL MODEL IS PEOPLE-ORIENTED

Hebrews 10:24-25

And let us consider how we may spur one another on toward love and good deeds. Let us not give up meeting together, as some are in the habit of doing, but let us encourage one another-- and all the more as you see the Day approaching.

Although it is unintentional, many churches end up using people like a piece of machinery to help keep the religious factory running. We bring people in and burn people out. Christianity in America has become just another enterprise. The church uses people as producers of goals, but has not helped them become the people of God.

Rather than using people to build programs, God is teaching us to establish relationships that build people.

The dynamics of deeply spiritual relationships have great influence for changing our lives. Healthy believers are grown in the context of genuine, spiritual fellowship. Establishing relationships in which we can live out the "one anothers" of the New Testament is vital to spiritual life and growth. (See Romans 12:10,16, 13:8, 14:19, 15:5,7,14; Galatians 6:2; Ephesians 4:32; Colossians 3:12-13; James 5:16.)

THE TRADITIONAL MODEL IS SELF-DEPENDENT

THE RELATIONAL MODEL IS GOD-DEPENDENT

1 Corinthians 2:4-5

> My message and my preaching were not with wise and persuasive words, but with a demonstration of the Spirit's power, so that your faith might not rest on men's wisdom, but on God's power.

I spent many years in my ministry thinking I was trusting God, when in reality flesh was my strength, knowledge was my God, and education was my goal. I was trusting in myself. My approach was to learn methods and apply principles. Now I am learning to trust God and appropriate power.

Many Christians have never experienced the power of God because they have constantly operated by the power of self. Until we learn how impotent we are, we will never discover how almighty he is. God wants to teach us to take our hands off, to take him at his word, and to take his assignment seriously. The work of God requires the power of God, which only comes from depending on the Spirit of God.

BUILDING OR BECOMING?

In the New Testament, the church is described as the Body of Christ and as the Bride of Christ. The church exists to become a healthy body through which the Master can accomplish his work and a beautiful bride so that the he can enjoy his people. Christ is the head, we are the body; therefore, we are to have a *living union.* Christ is the bridegroom, we are the bride; therefore, we are to have a *loving union.*

The enterprising spirit of our culture has caused us to focus on *building* the church instead of *becoming* the church. We have tried to organize the church into health and instruct it into beauty. But the one thing that will bring health and beauty to the church is loving relationships. The church is not to be a religious factory; it is to be a loving family. It is deep and genuine love for God and one another that will cause us to become the church.

In our city there are a great number of new homes being built. Building supply companies actually bundle all of the materials necessary for building a house into one package and deliver it to the lot for the builders. When we drive by and see that large bundle of materials, we do not say, "There is a house." It is not a house; it is the raw material for building a house.

When we look at all the people gathered into our

church building, no matter how many there are, we must not say, "This is a church." People are only the raw material for becoming the church. Ephesians 2:21-22 describes this truth:

> In him the whole building is joined together and rises to become a holy temple in the Lord. And in him you too are being built together to become a dwelling in which God lives by his Spirit.

We are to be in the process of becoming God's house. When his home is ready, he will come there to dwell. When people look at the church, they ought not to see our programs and activities, they ought to see God living in his house. Are they being drawn to him? It is not us they need, nor our programs; it is the Lord.

Is God at home in us? Is he at home in you? Does he feel more like a janitor, or the Lord of his house? Are we a healthy body? Is your part healthy? Are we a beautiful bride? Is your part beautiful? Are we a holy temple? Is your part holy? We must commit ourselves to seeing that the Body of Christ is healthy and that the Bride of Christ is beautiful. And when he is lifted up, he will draw all people to himself.

SUMMARY

This emerging model of relational Christianity calls for changes. It cannot be simply "added to" our old approach. It calls for fundamental changes in the way we approach Christianity and the church. *We must learn that it is not enough to come to church; we must be the church.* We are not here to fill peoples' heads with knowledge about God; we are here to fill peoples' hearts with love for God. We are not here to fill the building with people; we are here to fill people with God. Do not be deceived, "that which is born of the flesh is flesh, but that which is born of the Spirit is spirit" (John 3:6).

Many sincere believers are disillusioned. They wonder if they will ever find the life and love which God seems to promise. Others are burned out. They have been recycled through the organizational grinder year after year. Some have sat through so many committee meetings they have ingrown shirttails! Oh, how we hunger for freshness, joy, aliveness, and the presence of God.

A few years ago I came to the point of utter weariness and frustration in ministry. I was doing everything I knew to do, but nothing was working. During those months I would drive out into the country after the Sunday night service and weep before the Lord. It was there that God taught me my insufficiency. God began to reveal to me that nothing short of his spiritual power could really change people's lives. I came to realize that without his presence and power, it is all vanity. During that period of brokenness I wrote the following passage in my journal:

> Father, I realize now that people cannot be convinced intellectually or instructed mentally into your Living Presence. Only you can give

them that desire. Father, I am tired of preaching and teaching in powerlessness. I know it is my own fault, my own flesh that has done it without you. Forgive me for my audacity in trusting my gifts and abilities rather than you. Forgive me for my presumption that you would bless simply because I was saying something true. I know now that it must flow from you. Help me to understand your power, to recognize it, to rest in it. Help me to become a vessel that is pleasing to you. I have so much to unlearn. Teach my soul to possess more than my mind to understand. Thank you for getting me so empty that I am now ready to receive.

Later in the process, as God began to empower me for ministry, I recorded these words:

Father, the new insights into your Word, your power, your grace, your nearness are startling. I have been so shallow, so lacking in spiritual perception. It is as if I was blind and now I can see! Thank you sweet Spirit for opening my eyes, my heart, my spirit to your transforming truth. Without you I cannot even understand anything, much less do anything! Surely, Jesus, you have become to me "wisdom from God" (1 Corinthians 1:30).

I want to encourage you that God is in the process of restoring, renewing, and revitalizing his church. He is bringing people into the spiritual rest of finding their value in who they are rather than what they do. Being must precede doing. God is actively working to bring his people into the experience of being "strengthened with power through his Spirit in your inner being." God's time is now for you to "know the love of Christ which surpasses knowledge." He longs to touch you that you may be "filled to the measure of all the fullness of God" (see Ephesians 3:14-19).

The real, abiding presence of God can be cultivated in your life. You can enter into the living reality of the doctrines in which you believe. There you will find the Living God for whom you have longed.

The following chapters will reveal to us how relational Christianity can strengthen and empower our daily walk with Christ. They will also explore some of the fundamental changes in philosophy and practice of ministry which arise from the practice of relational Christianity.

RELATIONSHIP IS THE BASIS FOR SECURITY

4

Dealing with doubts about salvation is a common occurrence for many believers. For some it is a difficult struggle. God desires for his children to live with complete security and confidence in their relationship with him. We are exhorted to "draw near to God with a sincere heart in *full assurance of faith...*" (Hebrews 10:22). Every child of God can have that assurance.

UNRESOLVED DOUBTS

Unresolved doubt is often due to seeking assurance in the wrong ways or the wrong place. Many times, Christians who suffer from insecurity in their relationship with Jesus seek to comfort themselves with security blankets of religious information and activity.

I like to sleep in a cold room with several blankets on top of me. The layers of blankets give me a feeling of comfort, security, and warmth. All of those blankets may help me to feel better but they actually do nothing to change the temperature in the room. When the blankets are peeled away, that dreadful chill still fills the air.

When a person filled with doubts about their salvation seeks assurance by adding layer upon layer of religious information and activity, it may make them feel better for the moment, but the actual relationship with God is unaffected. What such a Christian possesses is not faith, but suppressed doubt. If he dares to examine himself carefully, or some preacher snatches away his blankets with a little hell, fire, and brimstone, he is right back to the same issue, "Am I saved or not?"

The fear that results from such insecurity can be quite debilitating. It will impede our spiritual growth and hinder our intimacy with God. After all, who could be intimate with One who, in the end, will condemn them to hell? Such fear and insecurity are favorite weapons of our enemy, Satan. But our heavenly Father has the perfect remedy for our fear: his love. "There is no fear in love. But perfect love drives out fear, because fear has to do with punishment" (1 John 4:18). The fears that hound us and hinder us, the fear of rejection, condemnation, and hell, are obliterated by the love of God.

It is coming to know the love of God that sets us free from insecurity, doubt, and fear. The pathway to security is a loving relationship with the Father. But many Christians remain full of doubts because they have taken other pathways in search of security.

SOLUTIONS THAT DON'T SATISFY

There are several common security blankets which Christians grab for security. In fact, when a person expresses doubts about their salvation, they are often handed one of these blankets by a well-meaning brother or sister in Christ. These things are not necessarily bad, but none of them will produce assurance of salvation.

1. REVIEWING THE PAST

Reconstructing the "new birth" experience is not the solution to doubts; in fact, it may be a hindrance. People who seek such a solution will then try to cling to a past experience, rather than to Christ, for their salvation. Imagine that you are at the scene of an automobile accident. The ambulance arrives and the Emergency Medical Technicians begin to give aid to a woman who was injured in the car. Frantically, she points to her husband who has not moved from behind the steering wheel, and asks, "Is my husband alive?" The medical technician does not say, "I don't know. Let me see if I can find his birth certificate." He does not examine an event of the past in order to determine life in the present. Instead, he checks for vital signs.

Vital signs can be helpful as a person examines himself to see if he is truly "in the faith" (2 Corinthians 13:5). Checking one's spiritual pulse can be done by comparing his life with God's description of his children. Does my life evidence the fruit of the Spirit (Galatians

5:22-23)? How has God changed my character to make me more like Jesus (Romans 8:29)? How has God disciplined me in order to change my attitudes and actions (Hebrews 12:5-8)? What is the Holy Spirit telling me about my relationship with God right now (Romans 8:16)?

The past event of salvation is not as important as the current evidence in seeking to relieve our fears. Asking questions about the past only adds to the confusion. "Did I say the right words?" "Did I know what I was doing?" "Did I know I was lost when I prayed the sinner's prayer?" Even if a person had the answers to those questions it would not produce assurance. Assurance comes not from your past experience, but from your current relationship with God.

2. REDEDICATION OR REBAPTISM

Rededication or rebaptism may be the prescription given that will "cure" a person's doubts about salvation. Neither solution will satisfy because they do not address the nature of the problem. Both rededication and rebaptism are human efforts to please God. They are man's attempt to purchase security. The problem is that security is not a commodity; it is a relationship. It cannot be purchased by any act of man.

Doubting Christians are often instructed to deal with the matter "once for all," or to settle the issue "right now." But the thing that is missing in the insecure Christian is not a "decision" or a "commitment" that will settle the issue. The thing that is missing is intimacy with their Father. You can't "decide" your way into intimacy. Neither can rebaptism "confirm" it. It is cultivated relationally.

3. MEMORIZING SCRIPTURE

Another security blanket offered to the doubting Christian is the memorization of Scripture concerning salvation. While such an activity may increase our intellectual understanding of security, it will not chase the fears from our hearts. Fear is driven out by love, not by information. Convincing our rational mind is the target of this attempt at security. But once again, we have missed the real Source of security, our God.

I am not against memorizing Scripture. I believe that it is a very worthy endeavor. But just as memorizing poems on friendship does not acquaint us with friends, neither does memorizing Scripture on salvation necessarily acquaint us with God. If Scripture memorization is done purely as an intellectual attempt to bolster our minds' belief in salvation, we will miss God, and we will seek to depend on the verses. However, the memorization of Scripture may aid us if it is used to relate to the God who wrote the verses. The verses do not save us, neither do they secure us, but they can point us to the One who does both.

Many Christians who doubt their salvation spend years piling up blankets of religious information and activity seeking to provide themselves with security. When times of severe doubting come, causing them once again to examine their salvation, they search through the layers of blankets, thinking one of them will provide their assurance. We get so confused looking for answers to our doubts that we forget Jesus is the "Author and Finisher of our faith."

SECURITY IS A PERSON

The first real step to security is to realize that salvation is relational by nature, not informational. For instance, racquetball is physical by nature, not informational. Some information is necessary; but until you get involved physically by putting on your tennis shoes, gripping a racquet, getting on the court, and hitting the ball, you aren't a racquetball player. No matter how much you know intellectually and understand mentally, you still aren't a racquetball player until you take the court, because the nature of racquetball is physical.

The nature of salvation is relational. Some information is necessary, but no matter how much you know mentally and believe intellectually about salvation, until you are involved with God relationally, you are not saved. You can have all the information right and still not be a child of God.

Since salvation is relationally obtained, it only makes sense that assurance is also a relational issue. Most of our attempts to relieve our doubts and fears are based on finding answers to our questions. *Answers are not the solution to doubts, Christ is.* It is not an answer about what a person did or did not do in the past, that will give them assurance. Jesus gives assurance. What we want are answers; what we need is God. We want a valid contract; what we need is an intimate relationship.

The key to lasting assurance of salvation is to get to know God so well that you can't doubt him anymore. He is the source of your salvation and the source of your assurance. Cultivating intimacy with God is the pathway to security. Chapter eight of this book will deal with cultivating our relationship with God. That relationship will produce in us the security for which we long.

A WORD ABOUT WITNESSING

Part of the problem people face as they experience doubts about their salvation is due to the way in which we propagate our Christian faith. Our rational mind and our focus on data have caused us to leave God out of the process. We need to refocus our understanding of the gospel itself and of the work of the Holy Spirit in conversion. Let me share with you three basic assumptions which I believe are often overlooked in our modern techniques of witnessing.

1. *The gospel is revelational by nature.* In other words, God must act upon a person's heart before they can understand the gospel. It cannot be grasped by the unaided human intellect.

In Matthew 16:17 we see Jesus respond to Peter's confession of his messiahship, "Jesus replied, 'Blessed are you, Simon son of Jonah, for this was not *revealed* to you by man, but *by my Father* in heaven.'"

1 Corinthians 1:23-24 teaches us that God is

active, not passive, in the presentation of the gospel: "but we preach Christ crucified: a stumbling block to Jews and foolishness to Gentiles, but *to those whom God has called,* both Jews and Greeks, Christ the power of God and the wisdom of God."

In 2 Corinthians 4:4-6 we learn that Satan seeks to prevent the revelation of the gospel while God seeks to make it known:

> The god of this age has blinded the minds of unbelievers, so that *they cannot see* the light of the gospel of the glory of Christ, who is the image of God. For we do not preach ourselves, but Jesus Christ as Lord, and ourselves as your servants for Jesus' sake. For God, who said, "Let light shine out of darkness," *made his light shine in our hearts to give us the light* of the knowledge of the glory of God in the face of Christ.

In attempting to share the gospel, we must do more than make a presentation of gospel facts. It is not enough to confront a person's intellect with information; we must confront their heart with the heart of God. Dependence upon God is essential in bearing an effective witness. We must be sensitive to his timing and activity. He alone can open the eyes of the human heart, and "it is with your heart that you believe and are justified" (Romans 10:10).

2. *Lostness is also revelational by nature.* A person cannot recognize their own lostness without the ministry

of the Holy Spirit. John 16:8 says, "When he [the Holy Spirit] comes, *he will convict* the world of guilt in regard to sin and righteousness and judgment...." Conviction is the work of the Holy Spirit in a person's heart. It is not the work of one individual on the mind of another. It is not our job to convict another person of their sin. That is the work of the Holy Spirit. Jesus said, "No one can come to me unless the Father who sent me *draws him...*" (John 6:44).

Sometimes we get so far ahead of God in our zeal for converts that we are in his way in the process of salvation. One day a lady came crying and knelt at the altar of our church. I asked her, "What's wrong?" She replied, "I need to be saved." Being the good evangelical I was, I immediately shared the information of the gospel with her. I noticed she continued weeping and seemingly paid little attention to me. As I invited her to pray and receive Christ, she made no response, but continued crying. Finally I asked her, "What is God saying to you?" Between sobs she cried out, "Repent...repent...repent." I was way ahead of God. I was trying to reap the full head of grain while he was still breaking up the fallow ground of her heart to receive the precious gospel seed. We must learn to *expect* and *respect* the ministry of the Holy Spirit in the process of conversion.

3. *Salvation is relational by nature.* People do not enter the kingdom of God through an intellectual agreement with the gospel. They enter the kingdom through a personal relationship of submission to the King. You do

not become a Christian by believing the right things about God; you become a Christian by receiving the living God into your life.

Jesus said in John 17:3, "Now this is eternal life: that they may *know you*, the only true God, and Jesus Christ, whom you have sent." That "knowing" is not as an admirer who knows from afar; it is the intimate and personal knowing of a friend. In fact, it is the knowing a child has of his Father. 1 John 3:1 says, "How great is the love the Father has lavished on us, that we should be called children of God! And that is what we are!"

Witnessing is not impressing people with the truth of the gospel, it is introducing people to the person of Jesus. He is the gospel, the good news from God. Our role in the process of witnessing is that of ambassador, priest, and servant. As an ambassador of Christ, we represent the gospel to the person both in words and in works. As a priest, we intercede before God on behalf of the person. As a servant, we listen to and obey the voice of the Holy Spirit, following his leading in the witnessing process.

The Holy Spirit is actively seeking the salvation of the lost. Conviction and conversion are his ministry, not ours. We must be available, sensitive, and obedient. Since salvation is his job, we must let go of the responsibility for the results before we ever begin. Perhaps no one has ever done so much to share the gospel with his generation as the apostle Paul. Even so, Paul never forgot his role in the process:

What, after all, is Apollos? And what is Paul?

Only servants, through whom you came to believe--as the Lord has assigned to each his task. I planted the seed, Apollos watered it, but God made it grow. So neither he who plants nor he who waters is anything, but only God, who makes things grow (1 Corinthians 3:5-7).

RELATIONSHIP IS THE BASIS FOR PURITY

5

Every true believer has a desire to become holy. When the grace of God touches a person at salvation, it immediately instructs them to turn from ungodliness to purity.

> For the grace of God that brings salvation has appeared to all men. It teaches us to say "No" to ungodliness and worldly passions, and to live self-controlled, upright and godly lives in this present age (Titus 2:11-12).

That happens because the Spirit of God comes to dwell in an individual at the moment of conversion, and God's Spirit is the *Holy* Spirit.

DESIRE AND DOCTRINE

Our problem arises when we realize that our

desire for purity is not enough to produce purity. We want to stop sinning, but we seem powerless to do so. We feel the desire to be pure and we feel guilty when we are impure, but that desire does not contain the power to make us pure. Desire operates through willpower. We choose, or "will" not to sin, and our willpower may set up disciplines to prevent sin; but when all is said and done, we still sin.

In our pursuit of purity, we sometimes turn to God's Word and we seek to find the secret to the doctrine of holiness. We discover this truth and that truth; then, we seek to apply them to our lives, thinking we will defeat sin with the truth. But, in the end, we again face the ugly reality: we are still sinners.

Ultimately, the conclusion must be reached that neither the desire for holiness nor a doctrine of holiness is enough to make us holy. No matter how deep the desire or how correct the doctrine, the power to be pure eludes us. The reason for this is that purity can only come from the One who is pure. The power to become holy flows from a personal and intimate relationship with the living God, who alone is holy.

THE GREATEST SIN

What is the greatest sin a person can commit? Is it murder or adultery? If the greatest commandment is to love God with all our heart and mind and strength (Matthew 22:37), then the greatest sin is to fail to love God with all our heart and mind and strength. Holiness is not so much an exterior righteousness as it is an interior relationship. You can be very good on the outside, but if you are not filled with love for God on the inside, you are still not holy. Holiness is not based on outward obedience; it is based on internal love.

The Pharisees of Jesus' day were very holy and righteous on the outside. They had external obedience. But do not forget what Jesus thought of them. He had his little pet names for them, his terms of endearment: "Hypocrites! Snakes and vipers! Blind guides! White-washed tombs full of dead men's bones! Fools! Sons of hell!" (See Matthew 23.) Somehow you get the feeling that Jesus missed his Dale Carnegie training. Why was Jesus so harsh on them? It was because they had turned holiness into a matter of legalism instead of love.

The purity that is demonstrated in our lives should result from a heart of love for God. In fact, it is our love for God that is the foundation of our purity. The legalist is not the one who is pleasing to God; it is the lover. The deeper, more real, and experiential our love, the greater will be our purity. Let me show you why.

THE PRINCIPLE OF PRESENCE

Holiness is a relational issue. God alone is holy and it is our nearness to him that makes us holy. The more we love him, draw near to him, and give ourselves to him, the more his holiness is reflected in and through our lives. Let's ask some very practical questions: "How do I grow in purity?" "How can I get victory over my sinful thoughts and actions?" Growing in purity, which means gaining victory over our sinful thoughts and actions, is found through what I call the "principle of presence."

God has some very important words for us concerning purity in 2 Corinthians 6:16-7:1,

> What agreement is there between the temple of God and idols? For we are the temple of the living God. As God has said: "I will live with them and walk among them, and I will be their God, and they will be my people." "Therefore come out from them and be separate, says the Lord. Touch no unclean thing, and I will receive you." "I will be a Father to you, and you will be my sons and daughters, says the Lord Almighty." Since we have these promises, dear friends, let us purify ourselves from everything that contaminates body and spirit, perfecting holiness out of reverence for God.

Verse one of chapter seven begins with "Since we have these promises." What promises? If we look back in the preceding verses, we will find God's promises that will empower purity in our lives. "We are the temple of God...I will live with them...walk among them...be their God" (v.16); "I will receive you" (v.17); "I will be a Father to you...you will be my sons and daughters..." (v.18). "Since we have *these promises*...let us purify ourselves." We should note carefully the relational nature of these promises. It is living in the reality of our relationship with God that will produce purity in our lives.

1.   DEFINING THE PRINCIPLE OF PRESENCE

If you observe small children, you will notice that when they feel threatened, scared, or hurt they will quickly turn and run into the arms of their mother or father. Why do they do that? It's because the *presence* of the parent *imparts* to them a sense of security, calm, or comfort. If you serve in the church nursery and you have a child crying and asking for its mother, it is not enough to say, "Your mommy is in the next room. Please stop crying." That child will not usually stop crying because you give them the *knowledge* that their parent is nearby. It is the *actual presence* of the parent that is able to impart what the child needs; it is not the knowledge of their presence.

Many things can be imparted to others through someone's presence. Have you ever been afraid, but someone was with you who wasn't afraid, and it gave you courage? We read war stories of how one man's bravery and courage was imparted to other soldiers around him. Through a persons' presence, there can be imparted to others many things which are needed, be it comfort, security, courage, or whatever. The power of a person's presence can change the way we think, the way we feel, and the way we act.

The presence of God has the power to do that in our lives. In fact, *the power of God's presence can even impart purity.* Think about the following scenario. What if Jesus Christ, in the flesh, were sitting on the edge of your bed in the morning when you got up to get ready to go to school or work? Then he says to you, "Let's get ready; I'm going to be with you all day today. Everywhere you go, everything you do, whomever you see, I'm going to be right there with you today."

Would that change the way you act? Would that change some of your attitudes, your words, your reactions to others? Would his presence impart a greater desire for purity? Of course it would. In fact, wouldn't his literal presence actually impart a greater power to be pure? If he were with you, wouldn't you have power to resist some temptations you normally feel like you can't resist? With Jesus beside you, you could turn away from some places you usually feel compelled to go. In his presence you could refuse to do some of the things you normally feel helpless to resist. If he were really with you, purity would be much more achievable.

The point is this: *he really is with you.* But, like the crying child in the nursery who is told his mother is in the next room, it is not the *knowledge* of his presence that changes us, it is the *awareness* of his presence. We all have a doctrine that Jesus is with us, but many have no awareness. As evangelicals, we have been told all our lives that Jesus is with us. What we must see is that *the doctrine of his presence doesn't transform us; it is the awareness of his presence.*

In fact, there is no doctrine we hold that has power to change our lives. Only the presence of God can change us. The more we can become aware of the real presence of God with us, the more every doctrine we hold will become a living reality in our lives. That includes the illusive doctrine of holiness and purity. The Jesus who lives in us is pure. His purity can be experienced and expressed through our lives as we focus our attention on him. Our normal practice, unfortunately, is to focus on the things we should and should not do. But it is not our concentration on the law that will purify us; it is our focus on Jesus. We spend our time trying to perfect ourselves. That will produce frustration, but not purity. We should spend our time cultivating our relationship with Jesus.

We cannot become pure by focusing on our willpower or self-discipline. Purity comes from transformation, not from education or self-effort. Our focus must be on the presence of Jesus who imparts to us his strength, his purity, and his holiness. Here is the truth that will set you free: *the more awareness of the presence of the living God you cultivate, the easier the process of purity becomes.*

2.　EXPERIENCING THE PRINCIPLE OF PRESENCE

How do we move beyond the doctrine of Christ's presence into the awareness of his presence? Knowledge of his presence is not enough; there must be an experience of his presence. Many of the things which God has promised are imparted to us only by the living presence of God. Here are several things which will aid us in experiencing the presence of the living God. (More will be discussed in chapter eight.)

a) Beholding the Lord

"But we all, with unveiled face beholding as in a mirror the glory of the Lord, are being transformed into the same image from glory to glory, just as from the Lord, the Spirit" (2 Corinthians 3:18, NASB).

Making time for silence and stillness, to simply sit and contemplate the Lord's presence, is essential. In our culture we have forfeited the presence of God to busyness, noise, and activity. If we are to regain the reality of his presence, we must deliberately fight against those things. Let me share with you an excerpt from my journal. This journal entry reveals my personal struggle as I was just beginning to experience the presence of God through silence and stillness.

I am so activity oriented. Busy, busy, busy; do, do, do. I almost feel guilty to stop. It's like I have a compulsion to "do something productive." Drivenness is at the deepest level of my being. It has sunk into my value system, my basic motivation, my self-worth. It cries out, "All this walking in the woods (times of meditation, reflection, and prayer), this quietness, is a waste of time. You are getting paid to work! Others will think you are lazy." Father help me to recognize Satan's lies and accusations. Help me to perceive the blindness our culture has created, which denies us of solitude, silence, and stillness. It is robbing us of you! Help me to remember all the times Jesus withdrew to a lonely place and he did it often. "But Jesus often withdrew to lonely places and prayed" (Luke 5:16). Help me to remember that you desire to lead me to "green pastures" and "still waters" where you can "restore my soul." Remind me that you built a Sabbath rest into creation. To deny it is to ignore a basic law of life. Help me to remember that you "rested" and "reflected" after every day of creation. Teach me to rest, not because my work is finished, (it never is), but because you commanded it. Remove from me the guilt and drivenness which prevent Sabbath rest. Remind me that amusement and leisure do not give "rest to my soul," only a brief break for my body. They do not touch me at the point of my need-- "restoring my soul." Silence and solitude realign me with you. They refresh my spirit, renew my mind. There I worship you, listen to you, and recognize your presence.

Silence and stillness will sow seeds which grow in your heart and produce the fragrance of his presence with you. Psalm 46:10 says: "Be still (or cease striving), and know that I am God." Get alone, get still, and get quiet before God. Don't ask God for anything; don't work on problems; think on his presence being with you and offer yourself to him to be his temple. We have focused on ourselves, our needs, and our problems for so long that we have lost the reality of God. We need to learn to focus on him. God is a person who can be known in increasing degrees of intimate acquaintance as we take time to behold him.

b) **Renewing our minds**

> Do not conform any longer to the pattern of this world, but be transformed by the renewing of your mind. Then you will be able to test and approve what God's will is--his good, pleasing and perfect will (Romans 12:2).

In Galatians 6:7-8 the Scripture reveals to us the Law of the Harvest:

> Do not be deceived: God cannot be mocked. A man reaps what he sows. The one who sows to please his sinful nature, from that nature will reap destruction; the one who sows to please the Spirit, from the Spirit will reap eternal life.

What we put into our minds, regardless of how innocently it may be received, is planting seeds that will reap a harvest. When we watch television that is full of sensuality, we are going to be reaping lustful and sensual thoughts in the next few hours or days. Even the appearance of certain commercials, in thirty seconds, will plant thoughts in our minds that will produce sin. If we read books that feed our greed or lusts, we will reap thoughts, actions, and attitudes that correspond. As we read the newspaper filled with stories of rampant crime, child-abuse, violence, and injustices, it will plant seeds that produce discouragement, defeatism, and depression.

The evening news can produce the same effect. I do not believe God intended us to bear the burden of every crime and catastrophe that is occurring around the world; but we are saturating our minds with it every day.

I am not trying to be legalistic. I am simply trying to point out a spiritual truth. The Law of the Harvest is operating whether we know it or not. I am not advocating the destruction of all of our television sets or the burning of all books and newspapers. I am saying that if we spent as much time seeking the face of God as we give to those other things, our country would be full of spiritual giants instead of spiritual pygmies.

I am not saying it is wrong to read a book or newspaper, or to watch a television program. I am saying we should discern carefully what we are reading and watching. I am also advocating moderation. We must cut back on the amount of information we are pouring into our minds which will give more space for cultivating a personal relationship with God. You may ask, "How do I keep up with what's going on in the world?" Let me make a few suggestions which have been helpful in my own life. I find that in reading the headlines and opening paragraphs of the first two pages of the newspaper, and by watching the first five minutes of the news, I am able to keep up with as much of the world as is necessary for me. God is able to handle the rest!

We should also check out how much of the music we listen to promotes a sensual lifestyle. We can't fill our minds with those things without reaping the fruit of them. Where do we let our thoughts wander? Over

what do we brood? On what do we set our affections--
things of this earth or things in heaven (Colossians 3:1-
2)? How much are we allowing unworthy things to
shape our lives?

"And do not be conformed to this world, but be
transformed by the renewing of your mind" (Romans
12:2, NASB). If we want to become aware of the
presence of God, we must wake up from our lethargy,
our unexamined living, our carelessness in spiritual
matters, and the influences of the world which have
robbed us of our sensitivity to God. "So we fix our eyes
not on what is seen, but on what is unseen. For what is
seen is temporary, but what is unseen is eternal"
(2 Corinthians 4:18).

c) Practicing spiritual disciplines relationally

Worship: When we worship, be it corporately or
privately, we should be singing *to* God, not just about
God. That will help to awaken us to the reality of his
presence. We must allow and encourage our emotions
to be stirred by love, adoration, gratitude, and praise to
God.

Prayer: Our daily prayer must become a time of
talking and listening. We have made it primarily a
matter of asking. Learning to listen to what God may
whisper to our hearts will help to turn prayer into a
relationship with a Person.

Scripture reading: Reading the scriptures
conversationally will aid us in recognizing that God is
with us. When we read one of his promises about peace

or power or his presence, we should speak to God out loud: "O God, I want that in my life." Talk to him about it. Share with him how you feel and ask him to change you. When we read of those things which are displeasing to God, then turn to him and pray, "Father, keep me from that sin. Grow in me a discerning heart and a spirit willing to obey you." We are not changed so much by submitting ourselves to the Word of God, as we are by submitting ourselves to the God of the Word. Learn to approach the Bible as a tool for conversation, not just a book to study.

Corporate life in the church: "Aim for perfection, listen to my appeal, be of one mind, live in peace. And the God of love and peace will be with you" (2 Corinthians 13:11). Notice that it is as we "aim for perfection" (not settle for mediocrity), and share "one mind" (not being full of division), and "live in peace" (not strife)...*then* "the God of love and peace will be *with you.*" The church that experiences the presence of God is full of people who love him and love one another. We should give ourselves to living in fellowship with other believers, not merely to share a building, but to share our lives. We are to minister to one another in "deed and truth" (1 John 3:18). We are to confess our sins to one another that we may be healed (James 5:16). We must learn to walk in unity, even when we disagree. The presence of God will be found in the fellowship of believers who are committed to being the family of God.

Journaling: When we write regularly to God about how we feel about ourselves and what we need to become more like Jesus, we give God another avenue through which to speak to us. If we will write honestly, deeply, and consistently, then the avenue is open for God to begin to visit us, speak to us, and change us. God said that David was a "man after his own heart." We should realize that the Book of Psalms is mainly David's journal as he writes to his heavenly Father, sharing with him his joys, sorrows, longings, and needs. Reading the Psalms as a man's journal can reveal to us the way to journal and the way into experiencing God's presence.

I will explore these disciplines in greater detail in chapter eight.

d) Opening ourselves to encounters with God

When we encounter the Living God it may not be what we expect. Isaiah encountered God in the sixth chapter of his prophecy and he cried out, "Woe is me, for I am undone!" Paul met the Living Christ and was struck blind (Acts 9). John saw the Living One and fell at his feet like a dead man (Revelation 1). God is an awesome Being. He is alive, present, and active. If we truly want to encounter the Most High God, then we must not cling to our preconceived ideas, our traditional viewpoints, and our cultural conditioning. We must seek him with our whole hearts. He promises that those who seek shall find. Earnest desire is a key to experiencing encounters with God. Remember, however, we are not seeking some experience, we are seeking God. Neither must we be seeking proof for our faith. If we want to encounter God in order to bolster our sagging faith, or to find evidence of his existence, we will miss him (Hebrews 11:6). That is a wrong motive and will not dispose us to a true touch from God. Encounters with God will not give you an unshakable faith; but they will plant within you the awareness of the presence of the living God. Encountering God will cause doctrines to become realities and knowledge to become life.

SUMMARIZING THE PRINCIPLE OF PRESENCE

While all of the above suggestions are helpful in actualizing the Principle of Presence, none of them are magic "cure-alls." They are all a part of the process of coming into a living awareness of the reality of God. It is the awareness of his living presence with us that imparts to us his holiness and purity.

In our desire to be pure, we have spent far too much time focusing on ourselves, and not nearly enough time focusing on him who is "altogether lovely." When we look at ourselves we are confronted with the darkness in our minds, attitudes, and actions. Sometimes it seems overwhelming. We struggle against the darkness that is in us, but we do not have the strength to overcome it. *Victory is not found by wrestling with our own darkness; it is found by turning to his light.* "God is light; in him there is no darkness at all" (1 John 1:5).

WALKING IN THE LIGHT

In the process of seeking purity there will be

times when we fall. What do we do when we are not pure? What do we do when we sin? When we sin, we should get into God's light as quickly as we can!

The Holy Spirit speaks to this issue in 1 John 1:7-9:

> But if we walk in the light, as he is in the light, we have fellowship with one another, and the blood of Jesus, his Son, purifies us from all sin. If we claim to be without sin, we deceive ourselves and the truth is not in us. If we confess our sins, he is faithful and just and will forgive us our sins and purify us from all unrighteousness.

The best thing to do with sin is to expose it immediately and thoroughly to God's light. Many Christians simply don't obey or don't believe God's word when he says, "If you confess...I will cleanse." A lot of believers remain under the power of darkness because they try to handle their sin in some way other than God's way.

Some believers try to *rationalize* their sin. They say, "Well, my sin is not so bad compared to others. Everybody has their sin; this is mine." Some try to *ignore* sin thinking "God didn't notice," or "It will go away if I don't think about it." Others (and this is most common for those who are truly seeking after righteousness) try to *pay* for their sin. This may be done by doing religious things, some act of self-denial, or simply by trying to "feel bad" over what they've done.

The problem we face is that we never seem to be

able to "feel bad enough" to deserve forgiveness. This is a trick of the enemy. This method will trap us in guilt and unworthiness, leaving us with a very shallow relationship with God. Do you know why "feeling bad" over sin will never bring cleansing? It is because the punishment for sin is *death,* not "feeling bad!" Romans 6:23 says: "For the wages of sin is death, but the gift of God is eternal life in Christ Jesus our Lord." Christ, not remorse, is the way to cleansing for our sins. He paid the price; he took the punishment for our sins when he died on the cross. The strength of our sorrow is not what brings cleansing; it is the blood of Jesus.

When we sin we must run into the light. We are to take our sin boldly to the "throne of grace." When our sin is exposed to his light, his light does not condemn us, it cleanses us. When we sin we should pray, "Father I come into your presence, sin and all. Here I stand exposing my sin in the light of your holy Presence. You see what I've done and I see it. I ask you for the mercy and grace your Son has provided for me. I have no other hope but the blood of Jesus."

Here is the key: *the blood of Jesus does not cleanse in the dark.* "If we walk in the light...the blood of Jesus...purifies us from all sin" (1 John 1:7). All sin is cleansed in the light of God. The moment we fall into sin we ought to run to God. We should make a covenant with God not to leave the room we're in when we sin until we confess that sin to him by exposing it to his light. Neither our sin nor our enemy can withstand the light of God.

Recently, one of our pastors shared an experience

he had just had with God. He said that he had risen early one morning to spend some time with the Father. In the quietness he heard the door open and saw his preschool daughter come over and climb up into his lap.

He asked her, "Honey, what do you want?"

"Nothing" she answered, "I just want to sit in your lap."

Then the Heavenly Father spoke to his heart. "Are you a better father than I am?"

"No Sir," he replied, "I didn't say that."

Then God asked, "Do you remember last night when you had to discipline her?"

"Yes sir. She did something wrong and she deserved to be disciplined," the pastor said.

"And now she's here sitting in your lap?"

"Yes sir."

The Father said, "That's how I want it to be with you and me."

That's how he wants it to be with all of us. When you sin, run to him. Expose your sin to the light of his presence through confession, trusting in the blood of Jesus to cleanse you. After you're done, climb up into his lap and tell him you love him. Then listen, and you will hear him say, "This is my beloved child in whom I am well-pleased."

RELATIONSHIP IS THE BASIS FOR MINISTRY

6

The word "ministry" means many different things to different people. Some view ministry as "their job," or "their profession." Others see ministry as "something they do" on Sundays. Many Christians see ministry as something which the pastor does. Most evangelicals have come to the understanding that we are all called to minister. But just exactly what does that mean?

MINISTRY IMPARTS LIFE

Ministry is the impartation of life. Jesus came that we "might have life, and might have it abundantly" (John 10:10, NASB). His ministry was giving life, eternal life, to all who would follow him. He told us in John 20:21, "As the Father has sent me, I am sending you." Our assignment is the same as his, to impart life to others.

It was the life of God which filled Jesus. It was

his relationship with the Father that allowed him to impart that life to others. In John 5:19-20 we read:

> Jesus gave them this answer: "I tell you the truth, the Son can do nothing by himself; *he can only do what he sees his Father doing,* because whatever the Father does the Son also does. For the Father *loves* the Son and *shows him all he does."*

Jesus again speaks of his relationship with the Father as the basis for his ministry in John 12:49-50:

> For *I did not speak of my own accord,* but the Father who sent me commanded me what to say and how to say it. I know that his command leads to eternal *life.* So whatever I say is just what the Father has told me to say.

Because of the intimacy between Jesus and the Father, the ministry of life was able to flow freely. "For as the Father has life in himself, so he has granted the Son to have *life* in himself" (John 5:26). The ministry of Jesus was to pass God's life on to others: "For just as the Father raises the dead and gives them life, even so the Son *gives life* to whom he is pleased to give it" (John 5:21).

The ministry we have is no different from Jesus' ministry. But if we are to be effective in accomplishing that ministry, we, too, must be filled with the life of God. That life comes to us only through an intimate relationship with Jesus. Listen to Jesus as he prays to the Father for us in John 17: "As you sent me into the world, I have sent them into the world...*I in them* and you in me." Jesus knows that this vital connection must be made if we are to touch this world for God. In fact, Jesus declares it will be impossible to bear fruit for him without this relationship: "I am the vine; you are the branches. If a man remains in me and I in him, he will bear much fruit; apart from me you can do nothing" (John 15:5).

Intimacy with Jesus is the key to ministry. *It is the depth of our relationship with Jesus that determines the degree of our fruitfulness in ministry.* Jesus is the "author of life" (Acts 3:15) and the "Living One" (Revelation 1:18), not us. If we are to minister life to others then we must draw near to Jesus.

GOALS OR GOD?

Our western society is caught up in the success syndrome. The thing that matters most is reaching our goal or accomplishing our objective. That same philosophy also fills the church. This has resulted in a generation of Christians who are working to "do ministry" in order to accomplish certain goals. These goals may be church growth or a certain number of baptisms or some similar measure of "success." When these goals are reached, that group of believers feels good because they are successful. They are satisfied with their accomplishment. In turn, they set higher goals for the next season of ministry. Other groups of believers fail to reach their goals, and they feel defeated, weary, or burned out. They may respond by committing themselves to "try harder," by trying to find someone to blame, or by deciding not to set any more goals.

In either case, ministry may or may not be occurring. The "successful group" may have operated their programs efficiently and many people may have come to participate or join their church because of it. But if the *life* of Jesus is not being imparted to those who come, they have not ministered to anyone. If those who participate in their programs are not becoming more like Jesus, it is not ministry. If those who pass through their baptistry have been connected to the church but not to Jesus, ministry has not occurred.

On the other hand, the "unsuccessful" group may not have reached their goals, but if the love of God has touched the unlovely, the peace of God has been given to the anxious, the hope of God has uplifted the hopeless, the forgiveness of God has cleansed the sinner, the comfort of God has embraced the hurting, and the joy of God has strengthened the downtrodden, then the ministry which Jesus gave them to do has been done.

Our goal-oriented mind-set often robs us of hearing the voice of our Father as he would whisper, "Well done, good and faithful servant." That is the real issue: *are we servants of God or servants of goals?* You cannot serve two masters. If our focus is on goals, we will end up trying to build programs instead of people. In fact, we will end up using people to build our programs. That is not ministry. Often, the result of striving after goals is fleshly service, pressure, and weariness. These things will rob us of our relationship with God and will diminish the life of God within us. *It is his life within us, imparted to others, which is true ministry.*

There is only one goal that is really necessary: *pleasing God.* Pleasing his master is the one aim of a servant. We are not called to be "successful" Christians; we are called to be faithful servants. Jesus said that the thing he always did was to *please the Father* (John 8:29). Paul declared that his goal was to "please him [the Lord]" (2 Corinthians 5:9). In Ephesians 5:10 we are exhorted by the Holy Spirit to "find out what pleases the Lord."

Great liberty will be experienced when we set our hearts on the one goal of pleasing God. Trying to achieve a multitude of goals and to fulfill myriad responsibilities leads to weariness, frustration, and burnout. We will each end up feeling like there isn't enough of "me" to go around. Besides that, we can't please everyone. Neither are we supposed to please everyone. Please God and relax! He is our Master. The simplicity of having but one goal, and that one goal always being attainable in every circumstance, will release a ton of turmoil and pressure from our lives. (See also Colossians 1:10; 1 Thessalonians 2:4, 4:1; 2 Timothy 2:4; Hebrews 13:20-21.)

MOTIVATION FOR MINISTRY

Many times we use goals to motivate people because we have not led them to fall in love with Jesus. We believe more in the power of goals than we do in the love of God. Using goals to motivate is simply obedience to the laws of our culture. Such motivation is external. The reason obedience to cultural laws is necessary is that we have not obeyed the very first law of God, to love him. The motivation of love is internal. Love-based motivation does not require the use of gimmicks, pressure, or hype. Love for Jesus is the only true motivation for ministry.

In John 21:15-17 we see Jesus seeking to restore Peter to fellowship and to ministry after his denial of Christ. Listen to his words:

> When they had finished eating, Jesus said to Simon Peter, "Simon son of John, do you truly love me more than these?" "Yes, Lord," he said, "you know that I love you." Jesus said, "Feed my lambs." Again Jesus said, "Simon son of John, do you truly love me?" He answered, "Yes, Lord, you know that I love you." Jesus said, "Take care of my sheep." The third time he said to him, "Simon son of John, do you love me?" Peter was hurt because Jesus asked him the third time, "Do you love me?" He said, "Lord, you know all things; you know that I love you." Jesus said, "Feed my sheep."

Notice the motivation for ministry to which Jesus is calling Peter to respond. He didn't tell Peter to minister to the sheep because he loved *them*. He didn't ask Peter if he loved the sheep. Jesus asked, "Do you love *me*?" "If you love me, then feed my sheep." Our ministry must be an outflow of our love for Jesus. When we are in love with Jesus we will see others through his eyes of love, feel with his heart of compassion, and be full of his tender mercy for those to whom we minister.

Ministry motivated by love will not suffer burnout. That is true because love "bears all things, believes all things, hopes all things, endures all things" (1 Corinthians 13:7, NASB). Any other motivation for ministry will fail us at some point, but "love never fails" (1 Corinthians 13:8).

THE CYCLE OF MINISTRY

Western Christians often go through the following cycle in their attempts at ministry. For some it becomes a life-long pattern from which they are never able to break free.

1. ENTHUSIASM: This is the initial experience of excitement, expectancy, and effectiveness when one enters a ministry endeavor.

2. STAGNATION: This period of ministry finds one still effective, yet something seems to be missing on the inside. The feeling is one of "the thrill is gone."

3. FRUSTRATION: At this stage one begins to

struggle with feelings of
giving up or moving on.
"What's the use?" becomes
the prevalent attitude.

4. APATHY: In this stage the motivation
for ministry is gone. The
basic mood is "I don't care."

God does not intend for his children to live under
pressures and burdens that lead to burnout. Jesus said,
"My yoke is easy and my burden is light" (Matthew
11:30). If that is true, then why do we so often find
ourselves weary, frustrated, and tired?

The apostle Paul was a man who faced great
trials and tribulations in ministry. Listen to part of his
testimony:

But we have this treasure in jars of clay to show
that this all-surpassing power is from God and
not from us. We are hard pressed on every side,
but not crushed; perplexed, but not in despair;
persecuted, but not abandoned; struck down, but
not destroyed. We always carry around in our
body the death of Jesus, so that the *life* of Jesus
may also be revealed in our body. For we who
are alive are always being given over to death for
Jesus' sake, so that *his life* may be revealed in our
mortal body.... Therefore we do not lose heart.
Though outwardly we are wasting away, yet
inwardly we are *being renewed* day by day

(2 Corinthians 4:7-11,16).

In spite of all the difficulties and dangers which he faced, Paul never seemed to lose his balance, his faith, or his zeal. What was the secret of his enthusiasm? The word "enthusiasm" is from two Greek words, "en," meaning "in," and "theos," meaning "God." The word itself is the key to maintaining excitement, expectancy, and effectiveness. We must learn to remain "in God."

MINISTRY AND FELLOWSHIP

One of Paul's favorite phrases was "in Christ." This was more than a doctrine to Paul; it was a reality. He lived with the *awareness* of the nearness of Christ, the power of Christ, and the provision of Christ. He knew that his competence flowed from God (2 Corinthians 3:5); his power flowed from God (2 Corinthians 4:7); and his necessary grace flowed from God (2 Corinthians 12:9). *The living fellowship between Jesus and his servants is the key to serving Christ without burnout.*

One of our problems is that we tend to separate our ministry *for* God from our fellowship *with* God. In our culture, we view ministry as our efforts to accomplish the will of God. When we give counsel to someone who is hurting, seek to meet the need of another person, teach a Bible study class, or do any other number of good things, we put forth our best efforts to achieve good results. We pray, plan, and work with the desire to produce the proper results, striving to bring about God's will.

Fellowship, in our culture, is seen as necessary times of refreshment when we can be with God, talk with Him, worship Him, or hear from Him. In short, we tend to see fellowship as the thing we do to get our "batteries" charged again. We feel like we must withdraw from serving in order for fellowship to happen.

TRUE SPIRITUAL REST

In Exodus 33:12-14, the Lord revealed to Moses how ministry and fellowship relate. In this passage God tells us how to avoid burnout and gives us the secret of true spiritual rest.

> Moses said to the Lord, "You have been telling me, 'Lead these people.' But you have not let me know whom you will send with me. You have said, 'I know you by name and you have found favor with me.' If I have found favor in your eyes, teach me your ways so I may know you and continue to find favor with you. Remember that this nation is your people." The Lord replied, "My Presence will go with you, and I will give you rest."

God did not say He would give Moses rest *from* service so that he could experience God more deeply. God said He would give Moses rest *in* his service so that he could experience and know God more deeply.

In our culture, we view spiritual rest as something which occurs only in times of fellowship. That is, we seek to rest when we have time to withdraw from ministry (i.e. in breaks between projects, people, and needs), or whenever we complete a job or task. Rest, however, is not the goal at the end of serving God. There will always be other jobs, goals, and relationships in which God wants our service. Here are the real issues: How can one have rest while serving? How can one have God in the midst of ministry and not just in times of communion? God wants us to experience his rest and his presence in the midst of our serving.

Ministry can sometimes be strenuous, inconvenient, or difficult. It may even call for suffering. But remember what God told Moses, "My Presence will go with you, and I will give you rest" (Exodus 33:14b). True spiritual rest is not found in escaping from ministry; it is not found in finishing the job; it is not found in getting everything and everyone straightened out. Spiritual rest is found in a *Person.* It is found in union with God. God told Moses that He, Himself, would be Moses' rest.

SPRINGS OF LIVING WATER

Fellowship with God is not separate from serving God. Ministry and fellowship are two sides of the same coin. Both ministry and fellowship are to be expressions of love. Ministry is love looking outward to others. Fellowship is love looking inward to God. Ministry is the stream which gives water to the crops. Fellowship is the spring from which the water comes. Our focus must be on our relationship with Jesus; he is the source of living water.

> "If a man is thirsty, let him come to me and drink. Whoever believes in me, as the Scripture has said, streams of living water will flow from within him." By this He meant the Spirit, whom those who believed in Him were later to receive (John 7:37b-39a).

We move into the second, third, and fourth stages of the burnout cycle when we begin to dry up due to emptying ourselves out in service. Then, we feel like we need to stop, retreat, and get filled-up again, in order to start the cycle all over. Rather than being channels of living water, we have become pools of information. Instead of trying to irrigate a field by running back and forth to the well with a bucket, we need to hold the hose which is connected to the pump which keeps the water flowing. That pump is our intimacy with Jesus.

Our motivation for ministry must come from our love for God. The only stream that will not dry up is one that flows from our relationship with the Spring of Living Water. Jeremiah described this same truth:

> This is what the Lord says: "Cursed is the one who trusts in man, who depends on flesh for his strength and whose heart turns away from the Lord. He will be like a bush in the wastelands; he will not see prosperity when it comes. He will

dwell in the parched places of the desert, in a salt land where no one lives. But blessed is the man who trusts in the Lord, whose confidence is in Him. He will be like a tree planted by the water that sends out its roots by the stream. It does not fear when heat comes; its leaves are always green. It has no worries in a year of drought and never fails to bear fruit.... Those who turn away from you will be written in the dust because they have forsaken the Lord, the spring of living water" (Jeremiah 17:5-8,13).

Notice that it is *living water. Ministry is the flow of God's life to us and through us.* Ministry is not informing others about God; it is touching them with his love, forgiveness, power, and hope.

DECEPTIVE PATHWAYS OF MINISTRY

Ministry that does not flow from an intimate relationship with God leads us down some deceptive pathways. These deceptions are sometimes very subtle and often deeply ingrained. In our attempts to carry out the plans of man, our minds are often "led astray from the simplicity and purity of devotion to Christ" (2 Corinthians 11:3). The Lord himself will deliver us from these deceptions as we turn to him and recognize his presence: "for it is God who is at work in you, both to will and to work for his good pleasure" (Philippians 2:13, NASB).

One deception that leads us astray is *focusing on*

the work to be done rather than focusing on the One for whom we are doing the work. We find ourselves working for God rather than in God and with God. The result of this process is that we begin to depend upon our flesh rather than God. When that happens, faith gets reduced to formulas and God's power is replaced by programs. This will eventually lead us into weariness and through the cycle of burnout.

When we are focused on our relationship with God, rather than our work, then we are more aware that it is God who is at work in us. Our strength is not emptied out into our work because we never leave the Spring of Living Water.

When we focus on our work, it seems as if we're never quite close enough to God. We know that we are serving him, but his presence always seems to be "just around the bend." We keep believing that we will find him somewhere down the road, but he doesn't seem to be near right now. The intimacy with God that we are longing for continues to elude us. By fixing our attention on our relationship with God, rather than our work, we will find that God is present now. As we set our affections on him, we will begin to experience God's nearness and love.

Another deception we face is trying to *rest in results* rather than resting in God. We strive to accomplish our goals, thinking that will bring us a sense of accomplishment in which we will find our rest. However, resting in accomplishments is not the same thing as resting in God. Any accomplishment, no matter how worthy, becomes an idol when we look to it as our source of rest. God alone is to be our rest. Jesus said, "I will give you rest" (Matthew 11:28).

When our rest is sought in results, our focus is on our activity, ability, and plans. When our rest is sought in God, then our focus is on our fellowship with him. God desires to be our daily bread. When our rest is sought in results, many times we will try to use God like a tool in order to accomplish our goals. God does not want to be a tool in our hands; he wants us to be a channel of his life. In being God's channel, we will find his presence, peace, and power flowing through us today. Our rest will be found, not in the accomplishment of our tasks, but in the presence of our God.

Another ministry deception that hampers our relationship with God is seeking to *please him by our performance.* Many Christians are caught in the trap of trying to please God by serving Him. It is not giving him your service with which he is most concerned; it is giving Him *yourself!*

When we make an offering of our work to God, we open ourselves to the fear of failure. If our work is not "successful," then we also face the fear of rejection. God does not want us to live with a spirit of fear. When we offer to God ourselves, we are not under the pressure to perform. That will enable us to be at rest not only in our work but also in the results. As we leave the results with God, then there is no fear of failure no matter what the results may be. When we offer to God ourselves, rather than our work, we can leave the results in his hands.

As we focus on our relationship with God, our

lives become channels of his life. Through that channel God can provide an atmosphere for growth, an outpouring of living water, and an opportunity for growth to take place. But we do not hold ourselves responsible to make anyone or anything grow. Results are not our responsibility, they are God's. (See 2 Corinthians 3:6-7; 1 Corinthians 12:4-6; 1 Corinthians 2:4-5.)

The pastor who is weary and pressured to "make his church grow" or to "get somebody down the aisle" has taken God's responsibility upon his shoulders. No wonder he is tired! When he learns to offer himself to God as a channel and focuses on his relationship with God, thus keeping that channel full of living water, he can rest in the fact that he is pleasing to God. The work is already accomplished. Whatever may result from that work is in the hands of God.

A believing wife who seeks to convince and maneuver an unbelieving husband to Christ will find herself frustrated because she cannot convince him or change him. She is drained of faith and spiritual passion because she has assumed God's part of the work. If she will concentrate on her relationship with God and lift up her husband faithfully in prayer, then 1 Peter 3 says that she can win him "without a word." By so doing, she is released from the pressure and responsibility of convicting and converting her husband, which is the work of the Holy Spirit.

Bible study teachers, deacons, and other ministry leaders may exhaust themselves trying to "make something happen" and still not have a fruitful ministry.

Fruit is God's responsibility; abiding in him is our responsibility. Jesus said in John 15: "remain in me, and I will remain in you. No branch can bear fruit by itself; it must remain in the vine. Neither can you bear fruit unless you remain in me" (v.4).

SUMMARY

When our ministry is based on goals, we will begin to assume God's responsibility. It is tiring and frustrating when we take responsibility for what only God can do. We are robbed of both spiritual rest and God's power as we begin to depend upon our own efforts. We simply do not know him well enough to trust that he will act or to believe that he is literally involved in the process. Our lack of faith keeps God at a distance. We vaguely assume his *interest*, but not his activity. Thus, we are left responsible to "make something happen."

Our relationship with God is the basis for ministry. As we learn to abide in him, cultivate the awareness of his presence, and know his nearness, then our lives will manifest the "sweet aroma" of his presence wherever we go. Unfortunately, we try to do so many things for the sake of our ministry. *But as we become intimate with God, we will discover that we don't have a ministry; it is his ministry through us.* His ministry is the ministry of life.

RELATIONSHIP IS THE BASIS FOR EQUIPPING

7

When Jesus calls any individual to himself, his call is always the same, "Come, follow me" (Matthew 4:19). When Jesus called the twelve to follow him, they knew the call meant much more than merely agreeing with what Jesus said. Jesus became their Master and their Teacher. The invitation of the Master to his servants is not merely to listen to what the Master says, it is to do what the Master asks. The invitation of the Teacher to his disciples is not merely to believe what the Teacher says, but to do what the Teacher does. Jesus said, "A student is not above his teacher, but everyone who is fully trained will *be like* his teacher" (Luke 6:40).

Jesus' call to us is just the same: "My sheep listen to my voice; I know them, and they *follow me*" (John 10:27). Our call is to follow Jesus. Following Jesus does not mean simply believing in his teachings. The call is to *follow after* Jesus. In other words, we are to follow in his footsteps. Jesus is not to be our hero; he is to be our *model!* Heroes we idolize; models we emulate. Jesus said it clearly in John 14:12, "I tell you the truth, anyone who has faith in me will *do* what I have been doing."

Jesus came into this world to incarnate the wisdom, character, and will of God. He proclaimed and demonstrated the kingdom of God. His attitudes and actions, words and works, were displays of God's will and purposes. He did not merely teach the good news; he *was* the good news! He embodied God's love and expressed God's will with both words and deeds.

His assignment to those who would follow after him is plain: "As the Father has sent me, I am sending you" (John 20:21). With these words, Jesus passes the torch to his disciples. Now it is their turn to incarnate, to flesh out, God's love and purposes in the earth. In the same way, now it is our turn. As those who follow after Jesus, we are now the body of Christ. We are to be the incarnation of Jesus to this world.

THE "WITH ME" PRINCIPLE

Jesus' method of making disciples is seen in Mark 3:14: "He appointed twelve--designating them apostles --that they might be *with him* and that he might send them out to preach." Jesus' approach to disciple-making began with a personal relationship with himself. While the disciples also received instruction, on-the-job training, and correction, it was the disciples' relationship with Jesus that formed the basis for their equipping.

Instruction, understanding, and knowledge in the ways of Christ are all good, but they are not God's final intent. *God intends that we become specimens of his kingdom.* The greatest key to being equipped for such a task is intimacy with the King. Like the early disciples, we too must learn to be "with him." This is possible because of his own promise: "I will be *with you* always, to the very end of the age" (Matthew 28:20).

The reality of the presence of Christ with us has been largely lost in western Christianity. The recovery of his nearness and living presence is what relational Christianity is all about. Jesus taught us that the Holy Spirit is the secret of knowing his presence:

> And I will ask the Father, and he will give you another Counselor to be *with you* forever-- the Spirit of truth. The world cannot accept him, because it neither sees him nor knows him. But you know him, for he lives *with you* and will be *in you.* I will not leave you as orphans; *I will come to you* (John 14:16-18).

These words are not merely words of religious beliefs; they are words of spirit and life. They represent an invisible reality that we must come to know and experience if we are to truly be disciples of Jesus. The real Jesus is with us. He is our Master, our Teacher, and our Model.

God knew that we needed not only a Savior, but also a role model. Jesus showed us what God intended us to be. We must cultivate intimacy with the person of Jesus through the Holy Spirit. As we come to know his presence and live relationally with him, we will find ourselves becoming like Jesus. In true Christianity, the "Word becomes flesh"; in mere religion, the word remains the word.

A PROPER APPROACH TO DISCIPLESHIP

If we are to effectively carry out our assignment of representing Jesus in this world, then we must be equipped for the task. Equipping a person for a task is much different than teaching a person for a test. Yet, our basic approach to making disciples is doctrinal education. When we stand before the Lord there will not be a final exam covering how much we know about Christianity. When we stand before the Lord we will answer to him for what we are *doing* right now.

> For we must all appear before the judgment seat of Christ, that each one may receive what is due him for the things *done while in the body,* whether good or bad (2 Corinthians 5:10).

We must come to see the process of making disciples as that of training a person to do a task. Our informational approach to discipleship conditions people to be spectators but not participants. The goal of many such disciples is simply self-improvement, not involvement in ministry. The kind of disciple we are making today seems to have very little in common with the kind of disciple Jesus made. Disciples who are not involved in ministry are simply not disciples. Such disciples are not followers of the Jesus who said, "For even the Son of Man did not come to be served, but to serve, and to give his life as a ransom for many" (Mark 10:45).

Much of the problem of our "uninvolved disciples" lies at the feet of pastors and other church leaders. We have simply not equipped "the saints for the work of service" (Ephesians 4:12). We have educated them, but we have not equipped them. Equipping requires "on-the-job training." We must create ways to involve people, not merely to inform them.

THE IMPORTANCE OF MODELING

Our Christian faith has gotten out of focus when we are more like fans than followers. We must keep in mind that our goal is not merely to believe in Jesus; our goal is to become like Jesus. The Great Commission, in Matthew 28:19-20, requires us to "do" all that he commanded. But Christianity in western culture has become *informative*, rather than *participative*, in nature. This shift has caused us to propagate our faith by educating disciples instead of equipping them. The process of education relies heavily on information, while the process of equipping relies heavily on modeling.

While Jesus is our Master Model, we should also recognize the importance of human models. If we are to raise up people to become followers of Jesus, we must change our method of training from one of informing to one of modeling. Information is a necessary part of training, but it is not the only part, nor is it the most important part. Many of our current discipleship methods focus on filling in the blanks with answers. Certainly, there is some good from such an exercise. But while answers may fill our heads with information, they do not necessarily fill our hearts with love nor our lives with good deeds. What we need more than answers is a model. Modeling is God's method of making disciples:

> Proverbs 27:17 As iron sharpens iron, so one man sharpens another.

> Hebrews 10:24-25 And let us consider how we may spur one another on toward love and good deeds.

> 1 Corinthians 11:1 Follow my example, as I follow the example of Christ.

Most of us can remember people who have had a lasting impact on our Christian lives. They may have been a childhood Sunday School teacher, a pastor, a youth minister, or a Christian parent. Somehow their life lit a fire in us which still burns. We may or may not remember the instruction which they gave us. But more than their instruction, their love for Jesus, their lifestyle, and their example left an impression upon our soul. That impression is more than information about God; it is something of God's life imbedded within our hearts. In some way, there has been an impartation from their life to ours. That is the power of modeling.

During my second year in college, I served as a

summer youth minister in a small town in Louisiana. In a nearby community I met a young pastor who was in love with Jesus. His love for the Lord was so magnetic I wanted to be around him at every opportunity. I never heard him preach a sermon or teach a Bible study. I knew this man less than three months. Yet in that short span of time, my life was transformed. His example caused me to fall deeply in love with the person of Jesus.

Models equip us for Christian ministry more effectively than any instruction we can receive. The stronger the relationship between the model and the disciple, the more quickly and effectively equipping can take place. Time and repeated exposure to a working model are important elements in equipping. The process of equipping through modeling flows like this:

1. DEMONSTRATING: In this stage, the model performs ministry while allowing the trainee to observe.

2. EXPLAINING: The model now explains what he did, why he did it, and how it was done.

3. EXPERIMENTING: The trainee now tries to do the ministry. This involves risking, failing, making mistakes, and trying again.

4. CORRECTING: The model now answers
                      questions as to why one
                      thing worked and another
                      didn't work. He encourages
                      the trainee, points out
                      weaknesses, and makes
                      suggestions.

A careful study of the gospels will reveal that this process was used by Jesus in equipping his followers. It is still the most effective method for equipping believers for the work of service. From our models we gain more than knowledge; we gain motivation, commitment, and ability.

Equipping through modeling can be done for all areas of ministry endeavor. It can be used in training disciples how to build godly relationships at home, in the church, or with others. Modeling can be done in equipping people to teach, to witness, or to minister to others through prayer. The process of modeling has a multitude of applications if we will but take the time to discover them. In the following sections, I will discuss some specific applications of the modeling principle.

EQUIPPING THROUGH SMALL GROUPS

As the Body of Christ, the church must be healthy if it is to manifest the life of Jesus to this world. The body becomes healthy by the "building up of itself in love" (Ephesians 4:16, NASB). The New Testament contains twelve commands that pertain to how we relate to "one another." The first of these commands, and the one from which all others flow, is the command to "love one another." The other commands all seem to be varied expressions of love (i.e. "be members of one another," "be devoted to one another," "honor one another," "admonish one another," "accept one another," etc.). If a local church is serious about obeying these commands, then it demands more than sharing a building; we must share our lives.

In order to equip disciples who are living expressions of the "one another" commands, we must involve them with a group of believers in which they are personally known, intimately attached, and individually accountable. Often, as a church grows larger, these qualities are lost. Without relationships in which we are affirmed, encouraged, supported, and confronted, we cannot take our proper place in the Body of Christ. A healthy church is the result of strong and genuine Christlike relationships among the members.

Small groups of eight to fifteen adults are an ideal setting for believers to "build themselves up in love." It is in regular interaction with such a group that "participative training" takes place. "Participative training" stands juxtaposed against "informative training." The small group must not become a place where we share a lesson; it must be the place where we share our lives. As we share honestly and relate transparently to one another, we will find strength for our weaknesses, hope for our trials, acceptance in our mistakes, and loving admonishment for our sins. The equipping of our character to be like Jesus can only occur in the context of intimate relationships.

Such living fellowship must be modeled by a leader who has a shepherd's heart. Christlike leaders, who model Christ's compassion, mercy, love, and acceptance, are vital to the health of small group ministry. Group leaders are not to be instructors; they are facilitators. They must draw people beyond membership into fellowship. The members of a small group actually become models for one another as they "stimulate one another to love and good deeds" (Hebrews 10:24, NASB).

When the individual cells are healthy and functioning, the whole body is healthy. When there is intimacy at the small group level, there is oneness at the congregational level. When there is accountability at the small group level, there is faithfulness at the congregational level. When there is love at the small group level, then the whole body will be "built up in love."

EQUIPPING THROUGH TEAM MINISTRY

Team ministry is an important part of the process of equipping disciples. Jesus ministered in the context of a team of twelve. The early disciples also ministered in the team setting. In Acts 13, we see a team of church leaders directed by the Lord for a specific mission. The ministry of Paul is couched in the context of a team who traveled with him. The church in Jerusalem, in Acts 15, relied upon a team for leadership and decision making.

Team ministry is the norm in the biblical records.

A well-knit team will bring effective equipping to the church, as well as continual equipping to themselves. The Bible teaches us that ministry in the context of a team has many strengths and great advantages:

1. Team ministry is God's method for equipping the church for service (Ephesians 4:11-13). The different giftings of the team members promote different facets of the life of Jesus being formed within the church.

2. Team ministry will cause ministry efforts to be multiplied. "And the things you have heard me say in the presence of many witnesses entrust to reliable men who will also be qualified to teach others" (2 Timothy 2:2).

3. Ministering as a team will allow more people to be blessed.

    > When he saw the crowds, he had compassion on them, because they were harassed and helpless, like sheep without a shepherd. Then he said to his disciples, "The harvest is plentiful but the workers are few. Ask the Lord of the harvest, therefore, to send out workers into his harvest field" (Matthew 9:36-38).

4. A team approach to ministry will increase effectiveness and bring added protection to those

who minister.

> Two are better than one, because they
> have a good return for their work: If one
> falls down, his friend can help him up.
> But pity the man who falls and has no one
> to help him up! Though one may be
> overpowered, two can defend themselves.
> A cord of three strands is not quickly
> broken (Ecclesiastes 4:9,10,12).

5.   The team approach to ministry will protect
individuals from pride. Our culture has
promoted the superstar model which has
encouraged the Lone Ranger approach to
ministry. Ministry outside of the team context is
open to greater abuse and error. "Where no wise
guidance is, the people fall; but in the multitude
of counselors there is safety" (Proverbs 11:14,
Amplified).

Team ministry concepts can be utilized at all
levels of church life. The youth workers, children's
workers, and preschool workers should be organized and
commissioned to function as teams. Church staffs,
deacons, and other leadership groups need the strengths
that are gained by learning to function as teams. Each
team needs leadership, and it also needs a sense of
oneness, love, and commitment to each other. Paul
describes the team spirit that is needed in these words:
"Make my joy complete by being like-minded, having the

same love, being one in spirit and purpose" (Philippians 2:2). Every team should pray, plan, and work together in close relationship. Their ministry must not only reach out to others, but they must also minister effectively to each team member. The health and unity of the team is vital to life-giving ministry.

Jesus promises blessings, provision, and his presence in the midst of team ministry. Listen to his words in Matthew 18:19-20:

> Again, I tell you that if two of you on earth agree about anything you ask for, it will be done for you by my Father in heaven. For where two or three come together in my name, there am I with them.

The very presence of Jesus himself must be the focus of the team. The ministry which the team performs is certainly important, but the team must never forget that it is not their ministry which matters, it is his ministry through them which brings forth life. Cultivating his presence, relying on his promises, and releasing his power are the keys to effective ministry. *Before a team gets occupied with ministry, it must be preoccupied with Jesus.* That team will "bear much fruit," but apart from him they can do nothing.

SUMMARY

A summary of the truths in this chapter will be helpful for those involved in the equipping process.

1.   Answering the call to follow Jesus means involvement in ministry. There are no passengers on the Lord's ship; all are members of the crew.

2.   The foundation of being equipped to minister is our intimacy with Jesus, the Master Discipler.

3.   Equipping disciples requires more than education; it requires participation and on-the-job training.

4.   Modeling is essential to effective equipping.

5.   A personal relationship with the model will increase the effect of equipping on the trainee. The deeper the intimacy, the stronger the impact.

6.   Believers can help equip one another through personal involvement in small groups.

7.   Team ministry that centers around the person of Jesus will serve to equip the team and those to whom the team ministers.

The process of equipping disciples to follow after Jesus rests on cultivating relationships. Our relationship with Jesus comes first, followed by our relationships with our brothers and sisters in Christ. In the context of those relationships, the Spirit of God will work to make us more like Jesus.

CULTIVATING A RELATIONSHIP WITH THE LIVING GOD

8

Do you ever feel like you're just going through the motions of Christianity? Do you ever say to yourself, "What's the use?" Do you think, "I used to enjoy this, but now I'm just tired?" Do you find yourself asking, "Where is God?" Are you sometimes afraid that your whole life could cave in from the pressure? Do you experience anger at God because you feel he's not doing his part? Has a spirit of weariness in well-doing been haunting your pathway?

All of these feelings are symptoms of failing to live Christianity from a relational basis. When we are not living in close fellowship with God, our Christianity can become a wearying exercise of the flesh. He is the power source in which we must learn to abide.

Serving the Lord over a period of years leads one through various stages of ministry. After the initial period of excitement, we may drift into a steady routine of comfort, or we may buy into a busyness which blurs our lives and leaves us very active but empty. In the first case, we often fall into a religious ritual without much spiritual reality. In the second case, we find our lives full of activities and events but without much spiritual depth and meaning.

Western Christians often find themselves in one of these two traps. It is possible to live this way for extended periods of time and never even realize our shallowness. In such a case, there are occasional vague feelings of guilt, or periodic thoughts that there must be something more. That "something more" is generally thought to be a little more prayer and a lot more work.

If we are ever to escape the ritual and the busyness, we must come to see that the "something more" is *Someone*! Until we find that Someone, and come to abide in his presence, our lives will continue to be lived on the fringes of spiritual reality. In the midst of ritual and busyness our lives become disoriented. Life becomes an unworkable puzzle with bits and pieces of "me" scattered everywhere. He is the only one who can fit the pieces together. We know this truth with our heads, but the experience is absent from our hearts. That is because our hearts are scattered out into our rituals and busyness and are no longer inhabitable as his home. We are no longer "home" to ourselves; how could we be "home" to him?

Yet that is what we are to be: *the dwelling place of God!* We are individually and collectively to be the temple of the Holy Spirit. Read the revelation of God in the following verses and look beyond your doctrine to the spiritual reality which they express:

> 1 Corinthians 3:16   Don't you know that you yourselves are God's temple and that *God's Spirit lives in you?*

> 1 Corinthians 6:19   Do you not know that your body is a temple of the Holy Spirit, *who is in you,* whom you have received from God? You are not your own....

> Ephesians 2:21   And in him you too are being built together to become *a dwelling* in which *God lives by his Spirit.*

God does not intend these and other similar verses to be mere statements of what we believe; he intends them to be our actual experience. They are reality.

As Christians we must believe, embrace, and experience that which is invisible. God tells us that he is the invisible God: "Now to the King eternal, immortal, *invisible,* the only God, be honor and glory for ever and ever. Amen" (1 Timothy 1:17). Jesus came to this earth to reveal to us the invisible God (Colossians 1:15). Now the Holy Spirit has come to make the invisible God real to us. Jesus, speaking of the Holy Spirit, said in John 14:17,

> The world cannot accept him, because it *neither sees him* nor knows him. But *you know him,* for *he lives with you* and will be *in you.*

We should ask ourselves: "How well do I know him?" The question is not, "How much do I know about him?" but "How well do I *know him?*" How intimate am I with the Holy Spirit? How well do I know his ways? How in tune am I with his voice? How sensitive am I to his touch?

Just think, the true and living God lives with us and in us, yet so few take time to know him intimately. We know a lot about him, but we do not know him. God is waiting to be known. He has made provision for us to know him, to experience him, to live with him in daily intimacy and companionship.

Paul knew the secret of believing in the invisible. He wrote in 2 Corinthians 4:18, "So *we fix our eyes* not on what is seen, but on what is *unseen.* For what is seen is temporary, but what is unseen is eternal." Our western, rational minds need a good dose of eternal reality. We have so filled our minds with the temporary reality of the material world that we have left little room for God's eternal reality. But God is there. He is there for you.

RELATIONAL ROADBLOCKS

In the following pages we will be dealing with how to cultivate intimacy with the invisible God. Our tendency at this point is to believe that we can read the rest of this chapter, gain some understanding, and then apply it to our lives, and the result will be intimacy with God. It won't work that way. Our basic approach is part of our problem. Let's examine some of the reasons why the following information is not enough to bring us into intimacy with God.

1.   What you are about to read cannot be learned by the instruction of a teacher; it must be *illumined* by the Holy Spirit. Illumination is a gift from the Spirit of God. It is the moment when our asking receives, our seeking finds, and our knocking opens the door. Illumination is that moment when the Spirit of God opens the eyes of our hearts to see clearly, to perceive deeply, and to be effected personally. When we receive illumination, something much more than intellectual understanding occurs. At the moment of illumination, the soil of our heart is turned up to receive the seed of his truth. If we will tend that seed, water and nurture it, the seed will grow and produce in our lives the "peaceful fruit of righteousness." Ask the Holy Spirit to illumine the eyes of your heart as you read.

2.   You cannot be instructed into a relationship with God; you must thirst for God personally.

> Psalms 42:1-2 As the deer pants for streams of water, so my soul pants for you, O God. My soul thirsts for God, for the living God. When can I go and meet with God?

No one can teach you that kind of thirst. If you are satisfied with your life and your relationship with God, then you will go no further into the depth of his reality. It is the seeking, hungry heart that finds God (Jeremiah

29:13).   In fact, *it is the depth of our seeking that determines the amount of our receiving.*

3.   The difficulty in finding God is not in what we have to learn, but in what we have to unlearn. Encountering the living God is not hard; it is just foreign.   The process goes against our cultural conditioning.   Our chronic busyness and ceaseless activity lead us away from the "green pastures" and "still waters" where the Shepherd "restores the soul" of his sheep. Unlearning busyness is not easy. We must also unlearn some of the biblical truths which we have understood only at a shallow and superficial level. Unlearning what we already "know" is also a difficult task. We must ask God to set us free from these things. Our God is able to do beyond what we ask him, and he promises to act "on behalf of those who wait for him" (Isaiah 64:4).

4.   As western Christians who are seeking to experience God, another fundamental flaw we face is our attempt to turn truth into principles which we seek to apply to our lives.   Our rationalism leads us to embrace knowledge. Our pragmatism seeks to apply our knowledge like a mathematical formula.   With this approach, the   relationship with God which we are seeking is seen as a *product* of certain information plus certain   activity.   However, love,   intimacy,   and companionship are seldom experienced by methods and formulas. You can learn all the right words and practice all the right disciplines and still not have a relationship.

God wants to be known personally, not deduced by an argument or cornered by a formula.

Even with all of the roadblocks which our culture and our flesh have placed between God and us, take heart! You are God's child and he is a great Father. He knows what each of us needs, when we need it, and how to give it to us. He will not deceive us; he is inviting us unto himself:

> Which of you fathers, if your son *asks* for a fish, will give him a snake instead? Or *if he asks* for an egg, will give him a scorpion? If you then, though you are evil, know how to give good gifts to your children, how much more will your Father in heaven give the Holy Spirit to *those who ask* him (Luke 11:11-13).

Our part is to seek him honestly, to ask him continually, and to love him fervently. Reach out your heart in faith to Jesus who said:

> So I say to you: *ask* and it will be given to you; *seek* and you will find; *knock* and the door will be opened to you. For everyone who asks receives; he who seeks finds; and to him who knocks, the door will be opened (Luke 11:9-10).

A SINGLE FOCUS

The believer who wants to walk in intimate companionship with God must stop focusing on things other than God. That is an obvious statement when it comes to focusing on things such as sin, money, or possessions. It is not so obvious when our focus is on ministry, church growth, self-improvement, or meeting other people's needs. These are all good things, but they must not be our focus. If these things are to be blessings and not curses, we must come to see them as *by-products* of our relationship with him.

The Christian who desires to know God's presence, his peace, and his power has to understand that his one calling is to please his heavenly Father. If we live our lives trying to meet everyone's expectations of us, we will never find peace, nor the presence of God. It may seem noble to try and meet everyone's need and satisfy everyone's desire, but in reality it is disloyalty to our Master. We need to decide: Whose servant are we?

When we allow our lives to be controlled by other's expectations and demands, *even our own,* we are headed for stress, pressure, and weariness. We will be driven to perform, to achieve results, and to become what others desire. We will be governed by our relationships and responsibilities rather than by God. In such a lifestyle, God will become just one more of those whom we are trying to please. When God becomes just another relationship which we try to manage in our schedule, the result will be added pressure, not peace. The promise of Jesus is, "Come unto me and I will give you rest."

It is time to refocus our lives on God. If God is truly our Master, then it must be his voice that commands and his smile that rewards. When our one focus is on pleasing the Father in every circumstance and in every relationship, then we will find our lives bearing much fruit. Jesus said, "The one who sent me is *with me;* he has not left me alone, for I *always do what pleases him"* (John 8:29). Notice that the reason Jesus lived in the presence of God, in intimacy and companionship with him, was that Jesus always did what pleased the Father. Pleasing the Father was the one focus of his life. So it must be with us.

Having a single focus of pleasing God will add great simplicity to our lives. Life becomes complex when we are ruled by a multitude of relationships and responsibilities. We are pulled in a thousand directions. We feel like we are running in circles because we are running in circles! So many things are left undone, which adds to our guilt and pressure, and robs us of our peace. This is the result when we are focused on goals, results, and expectations rather than on our relationship with God. In Luke 10 we find Mary sitting at the feet of Jesus, giving him her undivided attention. Her sister Martha is busily rushing about, trying to do all the things she no doubt felt like Jesus wanted done. Jesus said to her, "Martha, Martha, you are worried and upset about many things, but *only one thing is needed.* Mary has chosen what is better" (v.41-42).

The one goal of pleasing God can always be accomplished, in every hour of every day. There is no need to fret over the people we couldn't please and the things we didn't have time to get done. Did we please the Father with the use of our time? Did we please the

Father with our attitudes and actions? That is the only question that needs to be asked. If we are pleasing to him, what else really matters? When pleasing the Father becomes our only goal, then we will hear him respond, "This is my beloved child in whom I am *well-pleased!*"

Let me add a word of caution to what has just been said. We are not talking about a self-centered egotism that would use God as an excuse to "do our own thing." One thing worse than being controlled by our relationships and responsibilities is becoming our own god. That false, pseudo-spirituality can be spotted a mile away; it is really nothing more than selfishness covered with a thin veneer of spirituality. Having God as your one focus and pleasing him as your one goal requires true submission, humility, and a servant's heart. It means being God-centered, and at his word, willing to lay down your life for another.

When God becomes the center of life, when pleasing him is your only goal, you will begin to experience the nearness of his presence, the wonder of his peace, and the flow of his power. Here is the pathway to becoming God-centered: *passion for him...peace in him...power from him.* When your inner being is filled with the presence of God, you will discover that he is the Source of every resource you need. From his presence within you will flow "rivers of living water," expressing God's life to every relationship and in every responsibility of your existence. Rather than the pressures of life pushing in on us, we become channels of God's grace flowing out to the world around us. That flow of grace can only occur as we are filled with God's presence, because he is the source of all grace.

PATHWAYS INTO GOD'S PRESENCE

The door into God's presence swings on two hinges. One of these is *receptivity;* the other is *preparation.* Let's explore these two truths which form the pathway on our journey into knowing God. If we truly desire intimacy and companionship with the living God, then we must become receptive to his nearness and prepared for his presence.

1. RECEPTIVITY TO HIS NEARNESS

Hebrews 11:6 tells us that "... without faith it is impossible to please God, because anyone who comes to him must believe that he exists and that he rewards those who earnestly seek him." Receptivity to the presence of God grows from faith in this truth: God is really present with us and he desires to make himself known to us. Evangelicals have faith in the doctrine of God's omnipresence, but that is not the same thing as faith in God's nearness. *In order to know God intimately, we must cultivate a receptivity to the spiritual reality that God is with us personally.* Faith is expressed as we confidently trust in his promise to reward "those who earnestly seek him."

God himself has invited us to "have confidence to enter the Most Holy Place" and to "draw near to God...in full assurance of faith" (Hebrews 10:19-22). Being receptive means believing that God's promises *represent reality* and that they extend to us an invitation to *experience* what he has promised. Why would we be urged to draw *near to God* if we could not *experience the nearness of God?* God is not a doctrine; he is a life-giving Spirit.

God is urging us not simply to believe there *is* a "Most Holy Place," but to *enter* the "Most Holy Place." The "Most Holy Place" throughout the Scripture always refers to the dwelling place of God. Why would God invite us into his house if nobody's home? What kind of host would God be to invite his children into his dwelling place, but instead of entering his presence we were only given a textbook of information or a philosophy of life? God has not merely called us into membership of his church; he has called us into *fellowship* with his Son (1 Corinthians 1:9)!

Receptivity to the living presence of God is a *cultivated capacity.* It does not come with one prayer or even from one encounter with God. Receptivity grows from the seed of faith in the reality of God and the nearness of his presence. As we nourish and tend that seed, it will grow first the blade, then the stalk, and then the full head of grain.

2. PREPARATION FOR HIS PRESENCE

Every spiritual gain you make in life is a gift from God. Every gift must be received. In order to receive anything from God, a person must be prepared to receive it.

The gift of salvation will serve as a good example of this truth. A lost person cannot snatch the gift of salvation from the hand of God. They cannot pry it out by rationalizing; they cannot coerce it out by claiming, desiring, or agreeing. They can't pay for it by becoming religious. It is a *gift* which they must receive (Romans 6:23). But they can only receive that gift when they are *prepared* to receive it.

Preparation enables us to receive God's gifts. What is the preparation for a lost person to receive the gift of salvation? Repentance. When an individual repents, turning from self-control to God-control, then that person is *prepared* to receive God's gift of salvation. Until that individual repents they cannot receive it, no matter how much they believe in it, desire it, agree with it, confess it, or claim it. Salvation is a gift which a person can receive only if their heart is prepared to receive it.

Everything in the spiritual realm is that way. You receive when you are prepared. We need to be careful at this point not to fall into a very subtle, yet real deception. The preparation of repentance does not *cause* salvation. Salvation is a gift (Ephesians 2:8-9). Repentance does not produce salvation; it only enables a person to receive it. Think of it this way. Turning on a radio to your favorite station does not cause the broadcast; it only prepares you to receive it. Preparation does not cause God to give you his gifts; it only prepares you to receive them.

If you want to experience the presence of God,

then you must be prepared to receive him. It doesn't matter how much you desire him or claim him; you won't experience him until you are prepared. Experiencing the presence of God is a gift. There is no method to force him to manifest his nearness.

Our preparations are not tools which construct his presence; they are not methods which produce his presence; and they are not principles which coerce his presence. Our preparations to draw near to God are only the pathway which disposes us to his presence and enables us to experience his nearness. Living in intimacy and companionship with God is a gift. That experience must be received as a gift. It is not earned, achieved, or produced. But you will only experience him when you are prepared.

In Matthew 7:7-11, we find an interesting truth tucked away in the middle of a familiar passage:

> Ask and it will be given to you; seek and you will find; knock and the door will be opened to you. For everyone who asks receives; he who seeks finds; and to him who knocks, the door will be opened. Which of you, if his son asks for bread, will give him a stone? Or if he asks for a fish, will give him a snake? If you, then, though you are evil, know how to give good gifts to your children, how much more will your Father in heaven give good gifts to those who ask him!

Look closely at that phrase in verse eleven where Jesus says that the earthly fathers *"know how to give"* good gifts to their children. Think about that carefully. There is a "know how" in giving. The father has wisdom in the *giving* that the child does not have in the *asking*.

As my children mature, I give them gifts, not only for enjoyment, but also to instill in them appreciation, responsibility, and stewardship. Think about giving gifts to your children, not in terms of trinkets and toys, but giving them gifts which require accountability and responsibility. At some point we may give them a chemistry set, a car, or some investment money. Those gifts require a certain *preparation in the receiver.* You are no longer giving them gifts merely to enjoy, but for them to *mature.* When my twelve year old son asked me for a car, I refused to give it to him because he was not prepared to receive it. No matter how much he desired it, claimed it, or believed for it, he wasn't going to get it.

If there is a "know how" in giving that we exercise as earthly parents, how much greater is God's "know how" in giving what is good to us. God will not give us what we are unprepared to receive. The reason he withholds some of his gifts is not because he doesn't love us, but because he does. Our Father knows how easily we turn his gifts into idols, how swiftly we become enamored with the blessing instead of the Blesser, and how easily pride overtakes us in the midst of privilege. The experience of his presence is open to those same abuses. Preparation of heart is essential to experiencing intimacy with God.

Both receptivity to his nearness and preparation for his presence are cultivated capacities. There are things we can do which foster receptivity in our spirits and which till the soil of our hearts in preparation for the harvest of his presence. In the final section we will examine some of these preparations. We have briefly mentioned a few of these in a previous chapter, but we will now expand them. Remember, these things are not principles which, when applied to our lives, produce God's presence. They are the pathway which dispose us to encountering our God and enable us to receive his presence.

SPIRITUAL GARDENING

Cultivating the presence of God in our lives is much like gardening. While a gardener is absolutely helpless to make a seed grow into a tomato plant, there are things he can do which facilitate the process. While he is utterly dependent upon God for the miracle of growth, he is responsible to create an environment where the plant can flourish. The gardener must turn up the soil and soften it in order for it to receive the seed. If the seed falls onto hard soil it will not be able to take root. If the seed falls into shallow soil, with rocks or clay just below the surface, the same sun which God provides to grow the plant will instead wither the plant. If the seed falls into a plot of ground covered with weeds, the plant will be choked out and not grow to maturity. Sounds familiar, doesn't it? (See Mark 4:3-9,14-20.)

This familiar parable, which we have rightfully applied to the process of evangelism, can also be applied to any spiritual reality which God desires to establish in our lives. Everything in the kingdom of God works on the principle of the harvest. If we sow to this world, to rationalism, to pragmatism, or to the flesh, that is what we will reap. The experience of God's presence will be far from us by our own choice or activities, not his. But God promises that if we will sow to the Spirit, we will reap the things of the Spirit (Galatians 6:7-8). What are some of the things which we can do to prepare ourselves to receive God's seed, and to cultivate the presence of God in our lives?

1. WORSHIP

God is spirit, and his worshipers must worship in spirit and in truth (John 4:24).

The loss of genuine, heart-felt worship has contributed to the loss of the awareness of God's presence in our lives and churches. Our doctrines tell us that God is present, but we talk about him and sing about him as if he isn't there. God is there all right, but he is usually ignored. The Holy Spirit is very sensitive; he can be easily quenched or grieved (Ephesians 4:30; 1 Thessalonians 5:19).

Most evangelical worship services are pulpit-centered. The entire service revolves around the sermon. That is the focus of our meetings. I recently heard a pastor say, "We have exalted the pulpit over the throne." When we change our focus from hearing a sermon to meeting with God, then we will begin to experience God's presence in worship. Most of our songs are testimonies about God rather than expressions of love to God. We are missing a wonderful opportunity to obey the greatest commandment when we don't take time to express our love to God in every worship service. The presence of God will become real to us when we learn to focus our attention on him and express our love to him. True worship flows not just from the truth of our doctrines, but from our very spirit, heart, and soul, which were created by God and for God.

In our attempts to be "proper" we have become cold. We have shut off our emotions as if they are something shameful. *Our emotions are also a part of God's image in us.* They are not to be shut off; they are to be shared. In the emptiness of our ritual we call worship, we have become "noisy gongs and clanging symbols." Our lips may be saying the right words, but our hearts are far from him. Jesus says such worship is "in vain" (Matthew 15:8-9). We will not experience the presence of the living God until our hearts are prepared to release the adoration, praise, and love of which he is worthy.

To enter the presence of God without a spontaneous release of genuine emotion would be blasphemy! Study the worship passages in the Book of Revelation and see how God's creation responds to the experience of his presence. John falls at Jesus' feet like a dead man (Revelation 1:17). The angels are constantly crying out, "Holy, holy, holy" (Revelation 4:8)! The twenty-four elders are constantly falling down, casting their crowns at his feet, saying, "You are worthy, our Lord and God to receive glory and honor and power" (Revelation 4:9-11, 5:9,12,14, 7:11-12, 11:16). We find multitudes singing and shouting to him (Revelation 5:13, 7:9-10, 15:2-4, 19:1-2,6-7). God does not seem to be uncomfortable in the presence of genuine emotion; in fact, he likes it! Perhaps we should ask ourselves why we are so uncomfortable with something which God seems to desire.

We have been robbed and deceived by our culture and our enemy. We have so rebelled against the abuse of emotion that we have lost the genuine emotion which God deserves and desires for us to have. We have gone too far. If we will return to him with sincere hearts and allow the emotional part of our nature to be recultivated, we will be on the pathway into the presence of God.

In order to recover genuine worship we should start by offering ourselves up to God and ask that he make us into worthy instruments for his praise and glory. If we will pray to be worshipers, we will become worshipers. We are the human instruments which the Father has created for his glory and praise. It is the breath of his Spirit that will blow through us and play the music of heaven's love. Singing our love to the Father will draw him near to us. In his presence, we will experience the embrace of his love.

2. JOURNALING

A psalm of David. When he was in the Desert of Judah.
O God, you are my God, earnestly I seek you; my

soul thirsts for you, my body longs for you, in a dry and weary land where there is no water (Psalm 63:1).

These words were recorded by David in the wilderness of Judea. They record for us the earnest longings of a man's heart. They reveal to us David's search for God, his love for God, and his devotion to God. They are but one page from his lifelong journal.

Many of the great saints down through the centuries were keepers of journals. Thank the Lord that their struggles and insights, their victories and defeats have been recorded for our blessing. But we should realize that their journals were not written for our benefit; they were written as a part of a man's honest search for God. One of the reasons these journals are filled with such wisdom, insight, and inspiration is that God draws near to those who seek him, and he reveals himself to those who hunger after him.

Journaling is simply another avenue through which the invisible God can speak to us, guide us, and make himself known to us. Every point of access we give to God increases the flow of his life into ours. In the process of regular journaling, God will begin to make himself known through the writer's mind and to the writer's heart. Most of the insights recorded in this book are taken directly from the pages of my own journal.

Journaling should be a part of the regular pattern of our lives if we desire God to reveal himself to us through this activity. We do not have to write every day, but we must write regularly. If we truly want to meet God through journaling then we must also write honestly and deeply. It will do us no good simply to record the events of the day and the projects of tomorrow. A journal that is a calendar of events and activities will not draw us into the presence of God. Our journal must flow from our hearts, not our heads. We should record our longings, our fears, our hurts, and our joys. The most important things to write about are our thoughts and feelings about life, about ourselves, and about our relationship with God. Reading the Psalms as an example of a man's journal will help us to understand how to journal effectively.

There are some common hindrances to effective journaling. The first thing that must be overcome is the fear of being "found out." If we do not deal with the fear of someone discovering our journal and reading from it, then we will not write honestly nor deeply. For this reason, I do not believe it is a good idea to give our spouse permission to read our journal any time they want. We may want to share with them from our journal from time to time, but we must ask them to respect our privacy in the other things we write. Another hindrance is trying to write for the purpose of others reading what we record. A journal that draws you into God's presence cannot be written for consumption by others; it must be written for communion with God. If we view journal writing as a chore or task to be done, it will not be effective, nor will we do it very long. Our journaling should be approached as a time with God. It can be a time of communion as we express to God our love for him through writing. It can serve as a time of reflection upon our own lives, or it can be a written expression of our prayers to God. Do not worry about what form your journal takes, proper grammar, or style. As you write, just be yourself before God.

The use of a spiritual journal places you on the pathway for God to speak to you. Journaling will help tune your heart and mind to God's voice. The illumination of the Holy Spirit will come to you through journaling. You will also begin to recognize the presence of God. God is already there; he is just waiting for us to open doors into our lives through which his voice can be heard and his presence can be known.

3. DEVOTIONAL READING

Open my eyes that I may see wonderful things in your law.

Oh, how I love your law! I meditate on it all day long.

Your statutes are wonderful; therefore I obey them.

The unfolding of your words gives light; it gives understanding to the simple (Psalm 119:18,97,129,130).

Much of our reading today, whether it is reading

the Scriptures or modern books, focuses on information rather than transformation. We read in order to find out how to do something better, but little reading is done in order to be something better.

Reading devotionally is a discipline that opens the heart and soul, the mind and the emotions, to the transforming power of the presence of God. When light shines into a dark room, many things are revealed. So it is with the inner rooms of our hearts as we learn to read devotionally. Devotional reading begins with asking God to speak to us, to reveal himself to us, and to shine his light within us as we read. It is not merely our minds seeking to gain information from a book; it is our hearts seeking to grow in the grace of our God. Our attention is not focused purely on the pages, but also on the awareness of the presence of God.

When we read devotionally, we will enter into dialogue with God and ourselves. Such reading has a slower pace, a more reflective attitude. The desire to bring our "inner man" into contact, communion, and conformity to God is the heart of devotional reading. Informational reading searches for answers and techniques, while devotional reading yearns for fellowship and intimacy.

Cultivating a relationship with Jesus can be aided through devotional reading. Reading the Scriptures, Christian classics, and the journals of the saints are the best sources for devotional reading. God's presence and love are often made known to us through people around us. This is no less true of the authors of such writings mentioned above. They can become spiritual guides and mentors who bring us into a deeper communion with God.

4. STILLNESS, SOLITUDE, AND SILENCE

But Jesus *often* withdrew to *lonely places* and prayed (Luke 5:16).

Constant noise and the frantic pace of our lives are costing us intimacy with the Source of Life. God is found in the still and quiet places. When the Shepherd guides us, he will lead us to "still waters" and there press the peace of God into our souls. Only when we learn to "be still" will we discover the nearness of the God who is everywhere. "Be still, and know that I am God" (Psalm 46:10). As we learn to get alone, to get quiet, and to get still, we will begin to sense the presence of God.

Becoming aware of the nearness of God is akin to the appearance of dew on the grass in the mornings. During the stillness of the night, the dew is formed on the blades. God's presence is experienced in the same way. As we practice being still and quiet before the Lord, we will discover the "heavenly dew" has been deposited upon our souls. He comes in the stillness, silently and imperceptibly. His presence is not gathered in like picking berries; it is recognized and received in the stillness. If the wind is blowing at night, there will be no dew in the morning. In the same way, if our lives are constantly stirring up the breezes of serving, doing, and learning, we will not receive this deposit of his grace.

In our desire to experience the presence of God in stillness, we must not seek to be instructed, but to be watered, for we are very dry. There are plenty of times when we receive instruction, and that is good. But what most of us are needing is intimacy, communion, and love. These are imparted to us at a deeper level than instruction. They come only from his presence, and not from teaching.

Get alone for ten or twenty minutes a day and do nothing but sit still and be silent. Do not ask God for anything; do not pray with words. There are deeper levels of prayer than human thought. Do not offer God your words; offer him yourself. Allow a few spontaneous expressions of love to rise from your heart into your thoughts. Let them flow gently to the surface, but do not seek to grasp God. In the stillness simply allow him to settle on your soul. Let your heart be full of faith in the reality and nearness of the God who promised to reward those who seek him. Dare to believe that God is really with you and touching you. That faith will act as a magnet, attracting the Spirit of God who will come and rest on you.

Once we have developed the external discipline of stillness, over a period of time we will find that our hearts are becoming still, at rest and at peace. It is then we become fitted to be the dwelling place of God. When God is able to be at home in us, we will come to know his presence in the midst of our activities as well as in our solitude. Stillness can become an inner quality of heart that is carried with us always as we have complete trust in our Father and rest in his nearness. Such inner quietness truly brings "rest to your soul" and builds great strength in the inner man. God said in Isaiah 30:15, "In quietness and trust is your strength."

5. EXPOSURE TO AN ACCEPTABLE MODEL

> For you know that we dealt with each of you as a father deals with his own children, encouraging, comforting and urging you to live lives worthy of God, who calls you into his kingdom and glory (1 Thessalonians 2:11-12).

Finding those whom we can follow is an important part of entering into the presence of God. Those who have made the journey before us into the living awareness of God's presence are a great asset in finding our way. Without models we often get lost on side roads, discouraged along the way, or we may never choose to make the journey at all. Models convince us it is possible; they inspire us to go on; they help guide us along the journey.

Some who claim to live in intimate communion with God do not. Others do know God's presence, but their expression of that relationship is not attractive to us. Finding an acceptable model is important. That does not mean that our models will not at times stretch our faith, disturb our status quo, or even offend our minds. Learning to live in the awareness of God's presence is an adventure to be experienced, not a subject to be studied. If we are truly hungry for the living God, then we must have a willingness to let go of our old wineskins for the sake of tasting new wine. It may not be easy, but it is necessary. In Mark chapter two, Jesus offended the people of his day with his model of relating to God. When he was questioned why he did this, he answered by saying,

> And no one pours new wine into old wineskins. If he does, the wine will burst the skins, and both the wine and the wineskins will be ruined. No, he pours new wine into new wineskins (Mark 2:22).

A personal relationship with a model is best, but it is not always possible. Many people wanted to relate to Jesus personally, but not everyone could get to him. If you do not have a model with whom you can personally relate, do the best you can to follow. Observing another person's life, reading books, listening to tapes, and finding opportunities to be in the presence of godly models are all a part of learning to relate to God. The models we are looking for are not those who merely make great claims or appear successful or popular. The important thing is seeing Jesus in our models.

Lives that manifest the sweet aroma of Jesus are lives which are filled with Jesus. Those who display the character of Jesus are those who live in his presence. Men and women who live in his presence can lead us to live in his presence if only we will follow.

WRAP-UP

Cultivating the presence of God is the most important thing that you can do as a Christian. It is his presence that secures you, purifies you, works through you, and guides you. The Christian life is the life of Christ flowing through you. Intimacy and companionship with the living God is Relational Christianity.

Relational Christianity cannot simply be adopted as a new approach. If we create new structures, new methods, or receive new doctrines, but do not begin relating to God, we will once again end up weary, frustrated, and disillusioned. If you build a nuclear power plant and then try to operate it with coal as the power source, it will not function. We must be careful not to build relational organizations and structures and then depend upon them for results. Our total dependence must be upon God. If God fails, then we ought to sink. He is the source, the focus, and the goal of Relational Christianity.

EPILOGUE

For many believers, relating to God means finding God's will for their lives. Even the search for God's will can hinder us from entering Relational Christianity. We often treat God's will as if it is a commodity to be found and purchased or as a task to be done. We have failed to see God's will as an *unfolding relationship with Jesus* (see 1 Corinthians 1:9).

Knowing the will of God is the concern of every believer. Many Christians find themselves in times of turmoil, doubt, and even fear because they are unsure of God's will for their lives. As a pastor I am often asked, "How can I know God's will for my life?" Oftentimes, believers are searching, trying to *find* God's will. I do not think it is so much a matter of *finding* God's will as it is *receiving* God's will.

For this reason, since the day we heard about you, we have not stopped praying for you and asking God *to fill you with the knowledge of his will* through all spiritual wisdom and understanding (Colossians 1:9).

Our real problem is not one of "finding" God's will; it is one of being prepared to receive God's will. God's will is found, not so much by our searching for it, but by God illumining us as we walk with him. Better than searching to find God's will, we should find God. *Finding God's will is more a matter of developing a relationship with him than it is of searching for information.*

If we will cultivate a receptive heart and learn to live in his presence, then in that state of receptiveness God can illumine and reveal his will to us at any time and for any situation. That is the message of Romans 12:2,

> Do not conform any longer to the pattern of this world, but be transformed by the renewing of your mind. Then you will be able to test and approve what God's will is--his good, pleasing and perfect will.

The picture this verse gives us is one of a spiritually receptive heart. When our thinking is renewed by living in God's transforming presence, then we will live out God's will everyday.

If we seek for God's will, we may or may not find it. But if we seek for God, will he not also give us his will? Why seek the *object* when we can seek the *Source*? Why seek the *blessing* (knowing God's will) when we can have the *Blesser* (the One who willed it in the first place)? The Scriptures are full of promises that we can find God (see Jeremiah 29:13; Luke 11:13; John 6:37).

Am I saying that we should not pray about specific things? No. But I have found that one reason we struggle so much to know *what* God wants is because we don't know *him* well enough. *Isn't it strange that we so desperately want to know God's will concerning certain things, but we do not so desperately want to know him?* Is our desperation to know God's will an attempt to please him, or is it really an attempt to get the best deal for ourselves? Is our seeking God's will an expression of servanthood or selfishness? Is our seeking God's will an offer for him to use us, or is it our attempt to use him? If we are not seeking a deep relationship with God in between the "decision times," what makes us think we are being so spiritual by seeking God's will at decision times?

Seek God now. Get to know him now, in the everyday times. Then, when the decision times come, we will be much more peaceful and confident in our decision making. When we live in intimacy and companionship with God, he will be able to *"fill us with the knowledge of his will."*

God is so good, so incredibly patient and wonderfully merciful. And he loves you. He wants to be involved in your life, everyday. Knowing God's will and receiving divine guidance is really not all that difficult. The clarity of our guidance is proportional to the depth of our relationship.

Would you like a formula for living in the will of God? I know, you thought I didn't like formulas! But this is a good one; it comes from the Father:

> Trust in the LORD with all your heart and lean not on your own understanding; in all your ways acknowledge him, and he will make your paths straight (Proverbs 3:5-6).

MY PRAYER

Father, draw us to yourself. We have looked for answers in our methods and for power in our programs when what we need is you. Forgive us. You are the Spring of Living Water and we thirst for you. Grant that we might drink from the Source and not downstream where the water is muddied by words. Remind us that you are real. Reveal to us that you are here, with us. Father God, we are your prodigal children and we long to come home. Receive us by your great grace and tender mercy. Rekindle in us the fire of your life. May our lives be the wick upon which the flame of your love burns and thus bring the light of your love into the darkness of our world.

Lord Jesus, move upon your church by the power of your Holy Spirit. Touch your Body and make it healthy, alive with your living presence. Express your love to your Bride and wash her with the water of your Word that she might be beautiful in your sight, without spot or blemish. Come and revive your church, Lord. We love you, Father God. In the name of your Son, Jesus, amen.

If you are interested in hosting a conference on *Intimacy with God* or other topics, you may contact us at:

CALVARY BAPTIST CHURCH * 7550 CHERRY PARK DRIVE * HOUSTON, TEXAS 77095 * (713) 550-4323

For additional copies of this book or other materials, please write or call us at the address listed above.